The Witch of Edmonton

By

William Rowley, Thomas Dekker, & John Ford

ANODOS BOOKS
Candida Casa

Thomas Dekker (1572-1632)
Originally published in 1621
Editing, cover, and internal design by Alisdair MacNoravaich for Anodos Books.

Anodos Books
1c Kings Road
Whithorn
Newton Stewart
Dumfries & Galloway
DG8 8PP

Contents

PREFACE

THE Witch of Edmonton, which was probably first performed in 1623, was not published until thirty-five years later, in 1658. It was then issued in the usual quarto form, with the title: *The Witch of Edmonton*: "A known True Story. Composed into a Tragi-Comedy by divers well-esteemed Poets, William Rowley, Thomas Dekker, John Ford, &c. Acted by the Prince's Servants, often at the Cock-Pit in Drury-Lane, once at Court, with singular Applause." The best modern reprint of the play is that in the Gifford-Dyce edition of Ford, upon which the present version is based.

It is impossible to assign the exact share of the various authors in the play. The business of the Witch, the rustic chorus, and certain other parts mark themselves out as mainly Dekker's. The conception of Sir Arthur Clarington, and the subsidiary domestic plot is no doubt mainly Ford's. Rowley's share is more difficult to ascertain. The intimate collaboration of all three can alone be held accountable for some of the scenes, and indeed in even the passages most characteristic of any one of the authors, the touch of another often shows itself in a chance word or phrase.

The justification for the description of the play as "A known true story" is a pamphlet written by Henry Goodcole, and published at London in 1621, giving an account of one Elizabeth Sawyer, late of Islington, who was "executed in 1621 for witchcraft." See Caulfield's "Portraits, Memoirs, and Characters of Remarkable Persons," 1794. No existing copy of the pamphlet is known, but the British Museum possesses copies of two of Goodcole's other pamphlets on similar subjects.

PROLOGUE

The town of Edmonton hath lent the stage
A Devil[1] and a Witch, both in an age.
To make comparisons it were uncivil
Between so even a pair, a Witch and Devil;
But as the year doth with his plenty bring
As well a latter as a former spring,
So hath this Witch enjoyed the first, and reason
Presumes she may partake the other season:
In acts deserving name, the proverb says,
"Once good, and ever;" why not so in plays?
Why not in this? since, gentlemen, we flatter
No expectation; here is mirth and matter.

MASTER BIRD.

The whole argument of the play is this distich.

Forced marriage, murder; murder blood requires:
Reproach, revenge; revenge hell's help desires.

[1]An allusion to the popular old play of *The Merry Devil of Edmonton*, written about twenty years previously.

DRAMATIS PERSONAE

Sir Arthur Clarington.
Old Thorney, a Gentleman.
Carter, a Rich Yeoman.

Warbeck, } Suitors To Carter's Daughters.
Somerton, }

Frank, Thorney's Son.
Old Banks, a Countryman.
Cuddy Banks, his Son.

Ratcliffe, } Countrymen.
Hamluc, }

Morris-dancers.
Sawgut, an old Fiddler.
A Dog, a Familiar.
A Spirit.
Countrymen, Justice, Constable, Officers, Serving-men and Maids.

Mother Sawyer, the Witch.
Ann, Ratcliffe's Wife.

Susan, } Carter's Daughters.
Katherine, }

Winnifred, Sir Arthur's Maid.

SCENE—The town and neighbourhood of Edmonton; in the end of the last act, London.

ACT THE FIRST.

SCENE I.—*The neighbourhood of Edmonton. A Room in the House of Sir* ARTHUR CLARINGTON.

Enter FRANK THORNEY *and* WINNIFRED, *who is with child.*

FRANK. Come, wench; why, here's a business soon dispatched:
Thy heart I know is now at ease; thou need'st not
Fear what the tattling gossips in their cups
Can speak against thy fame; thy child shall know
Whom to call dad now.

Win. You have here discharged
The true part of an honest man; I cannot
Request a fuller satisfaction
Than you have freely granted: yet methinks
'Tis an hard case, being lawful man and wife,
We should not live together.

Frank. Had I failed
In promise of my truth to thee, we must
Have then been ever sundered; now the longest
Of our forbearing either's company
Is only but to gain a little time
For our continuing thrift; that so hereafter
The heir that shall be born may not have cause
To curse his hour of birth, which made him feel
The misery of beggary and want,—
Two devils that are occasions to enforce
A shameful end. My plots aim but to keep
My father's love.

Win. And that will be as difficult
To be preserved, when he shall understand
How you are married, as it will be now,
Should you confess it to him.

Frank. Fathers are
Won by degrees, not bluntly, as our masters
Or wrongèd friends are; and besides I'll use
Such dutiful and ready means, that ere
He can have notice of what's past, th' inheritance

To which I am born heir shall be assured;
That done, why, let him know it: if he like it not,
Yet he shall have no power in him left
To cross the thriving of it.

Win. You who had
The conquest of my maiden-love may easily
Conquer the fears of my distrust. And whither
Must I be hurried?

Frank. Prithee do not use
A word so much unsuitable to the constant
Affections of thy husband: thou shalt live
Near Waltham Abbey with thy uncle Selman;
I have acquainted him with all at large:
He'll use thee kindly; thou shalt want no pleasures,
Nor any other fit supplies whatever
Thou canst in heart desire.

Win. All these are nothing
Without your company.

Frank. Which thou shalt have
Once every month at least.

Win. Once every month!
Is this to have an husband?

Frank. Perhaps oftener;
That's as occasion serves.

Win. Ay, ay; in case
No other beauty tempt your eye, whom you
Like better, I may chance to be remembered,
And see you now and then. Faith, I did hope
You'd not have used me so: 'tis but my fortune.
And yet, if not for my sake, have some pity
Upon the child I go with; that's your own:
And 'less you'll be a cruel-hearted father,
You cannot but remember that.
Heaven knows how—

Frank. To quit which fear at once,
As by the ceremony late performed
I plighted thee a faith as free from challenge

As any double thought; once more, in hearing
Of Heaven and thee, I vow that never henceforth
Disgrace, reproof, lawless affections, threats,
Or what can be suggested 'gainst our marriage,
Shall cause me falsify that bridal oath
That binds me thine. And, Winnifred, whenever
The wanton heat of youth, by subtle baits
Of beauty, or what woman's art can practise,
Draw me from only loving thee, let Heaven
Inflict upon my life some fearful ruin!
I hope thou dost believe me.

Win. Swear no more;
I am confirmed, and will resolve to do
What you think most behoveful for us.

Frank. Thus, then;
Make thyself ready; at the furthest house
Upon the green without the town, your uncle
Expects you. For a little time, farewell!

Win. Sweet,
We shall meet again as soon as thou canst possibly?

Frank. We shall. One kiss—away! [*Exit* WINNIFRED.

Enter SIR ARTHUR CLARINGTON.

Sir Arth. Frank Thorney!

Frank. Here, sir.

Sir Arth. Alone? then must I tell thee in plain terms
Thou hast wronged thy master's house basely and lewdly.

Frank. Your house, sir?

Sir Arth. Yes, sir: if the nimble devil
That wantoned in your blood rebelled against
All rules of honest duty, you might, sir,
Have found out some more fitting place than here
To have built a stews in. All the country whispers
How shamefully thou hast undone a maid,
Approved for modest life, for civil carriage,
Till thy prevailing perjuries enticed her
To forfeit shame. Will you be honest yet,

Make her amends and marry her?

Frank. So, sir,
I might bring both myself and her to beggary;
And that would be a shame worse than the other.

Sir Arth. You should have thought on this before, and then
Your reason would have overswayed the passion
Of your unruly lust. But that you may
Be left without excuse, to salve the infamy
Of my disgracèd house, and 'cause you are
A gentleman, and both of you my servants,
I'll make the maid a portion.

Frank. So you promised me
Before, in case I married her. I know
Sir Arthur Clarington deserves the credit
Report hath lent him, and presume you are
A debtor to your promise: but upon
What certainty shall I resolve? Excuse me
For being somewhat rude.

Sir Arth. It is but reason.
Well, Frank, what think'st thou of two hundred pounds
And a continual friend?

Frank. Though my poor fortunes
Might happily prefer me to a choice
Of a far greater portion, yet, to right
A wrongèd maid and to preserve your favour,
I am content to accept your proffer.

Sir Arth. Art thou?

Frank. Sir, we shall every day have need to employ
The use of what you please to give.

Sir Arth. Thou shall have't.

Frank. Then I claim
Your promise.—We are man and wife.

Sir Arth. Already?

Frank. And more than so, sir, I have promised her
Free entertainment in her uncle's house

Near Waltham Abbey, where she may securely
Sojourn, till time and my endeavours work
My father's love and liking.

Sir Arth. Honest Frank!

Frank. I hope, sir, you will think I cannot keep her
Without a daily charge.

Sir Arth. As for the money,
'Tis all thine own! and though I cannot make thee
A present payment, yet thou shalt be sure
I will not fail thee.

Frank. But our occasions—

Sir Arth. Nay, nay,
Talk not of your occasions; trust my bounty;
It shall not sleep.—Hast married her, i'faith, Frank?
'Tis well, 'tis passing well!—then, Winnifred,
Once more thou art an honest woman. Frank,
Thou hast a jewel; love her; she'll deserve it.
And when to Waltham?

Frank. She is making ready;
Her uncle stays for her.

Sir Arth. Most provident speed.
Frank, I will be thy friend, and such a friend!—
Thou'lt bring her thither?

Frank. Sir, I cannot; newly
My father sent me word I should come to him.

Sir Arth. Marry, and do; I know thou hast a wit
To handle him.

Frank. I have a suit t'ye.

Sir Arth. What is't?
Anything, Frank; command it.

Frank. That you'll please
By letters to assure my father that
I am not married.

Sir Arth. How!

Frank. Some one or other
Hath certainly informed him that I purposed
To marry Winnifred; on which he threatened
To disinherit me:—to prevent it,
Lowly I crave your letters, which he seeing
Will credit; and I hope, ere I return,
On such conditions as I'll frame, his lands
Shall be assured.

Sir Arth. But what is there to quit[2]
My knowledge of the marriage?

Frank. Why, you were not
A witness to it.

Sir Arth. I conceive; and then—
His land confirmed, thou wilt acquaint him throughly
With all that's past.

Frank. I mean no less.

Sir Arth. Provided
I never was made privy to't.

Frank. Alas, sir,
Am I a talker?

Sir Arth. Draw thyself the letter,
I'll put my hand to't. I commend thy policy;
Thou'rt witty, witty, Frank; nay, nay, 'tis fit:
Dispatch it.

Frank. I shall write effectually. [*Exit.*

Sir Arth. Go thy way, cuckoo;—have I caught the young man?
One trouble, then, is freed. He that will feast
At other's cost must be a bold-faced guest.

Re-enter WINNIFRED *in a riding-suit.*

Win, I have heard the news; all now is safe;
The worst is past: thy lip, wench [*Kisses her*]: I must bid
Farewell, for fashion's sake; but I will visit thee

[2] *i.e.* Acquit.

Suddenly, girl. This was cleanly carried;
Ha! was't not, Win?

Win. Then were my happiness,
That I in heart repent I did not bring him
The dower of a virginity. Sir, forgive me;
I have been much to blame: had not my lewdness[3]
Given way to your immoderate waste of virtue,
You had not with such eagerness pursued
The error of your goodness.

Sir Arth. Dear, dear Win,
I hug this art of thine; it shows how cleanly
Thou canst beguile, in case occasion serve
To practise; it becomes thee: now we share
Free scope enough, without control or fear,
To interchange our pleasures; we will surfeit
In our embraces, wench. Come, tell me, when
Wilt thou appoint a meeting?

Win. What to do?

Sir Arth. Good, good, to con the lesson of our loves,
Our secret game.

Win. O, blush to speak it further!
As you're a noble gentleman, forget
A sin so monstrous: 'tis not gently done
To open a cured wound: I know you speak
For trial; 'troth, you need not.

Sir Arth. I for trial?
Not I, by this good sunshine!

Win. Can you name
That syllable of good, and yet not tremble
To think to what a foul and black intent
You use it for an oath? Let me resolve[4] you:
If you appear in any visitation
That brings not with it pity for the wrongs
Done to abusèd Thorney, my kind husband,—

[3]This speech is very corrupt. Dyce suggested "lewdness" in place of the "laundress" of the old edition.

[4]Assure.

If you infect mine ear with any breath
That is not thoroughly perfumed with sighs
For former deeds of lust,—may I be cursed
Even in my prayers, when I vouchsafe
To see or hear you! I will change my life
From a loose whore to a repentant wife.

Sir Arth. Wilt thou turn monster now? art not ashamed
After so many months to be honest at last?
Away, away! fie on't!

Win. My resolution
Is built upon a rock. This very day
Young Thorney vowed, with oaths not to be doubted,
That never any change of love should cancel
The bonds in which we are to either bound
Of lasting truth: and shall I, then, for my part
Unfile the sacred oath set on record
In Heaven's book? Sir Arthur, do not study
To add to your lascivious lust the sin
Of sacrilege; for if you but endeavour
By any unchaste word to tempt my constancy
You strive as much as in you lies to ruin
A temple hallowed to the purity
Of holy marriage. I have said enough;
You may believe me.

Sir Arth. Get you to your nunnery;
There freeze in your cold cloister: this is fine!

Win. Good angels guide me! Sir, you'll give me leave
To weep and pray for your conversion?

Sir Arth. Yes:
Away to Waltham! Pox on your honesty!
Had you no other trick to fool me? well,
You may want money yet.

Win. None that I'll send for
To you, for hire of a damnation.
When I am gone, think on my just complaint:
I was your devil; O, be you my saint! [*Exit.*

Sir Arth. Go, go thy ways; as changeable a baggage
As ever cozened knight: I'm glad I'm rid of her.

Honest! marry, hang her! Thorney is my debtor;
I thought to have paid him too; but fools have fortune. [*Exit.*

SCENE II.—*Edmonton. A Room in* CARTER'S *House.*

Enter OLD THORNEY *and* CARTER.

O. Thor. You offer, Master Carter, like a gentleman; I cannot find fault with it, 'tis so fair.

Car. No gentleman I, Master Thorney; spare the Mastership, call me by my name, John Carter. Master is a title my father, nor his before him, were acquainted with; honest Hertfordshire yeomen; such an one am I; my word and my deed shall be proved one at all times. I mean to give you no security for the marriage money.

O. Thor. How! no security? although it need not so long as you live, yet who is he has surety of his life one hour? Men, the proverb says, are mortal; else, for my part, I distrust you not, were the sum double.

Car. Double, treble, more or less, I tell you, Master Thorney, I'll give no security. Bonds and bills are but terriers to catch fools, and keep lazy knaves busy; my security shall be present payment. And we here about Edmonton hold present payment as sure as an alderman's bond in London, Master Thorney.

O. Thor. I cry you mercy, sir; I understood you not.

Car. I like young Frank well, so does my Susan too; the girl has a fancy to him, which makes me ready in my purse. There be other suitors within, that make much noise to little purpose. If Frank love Sue, Sue shall have none but Frank. 'Tis a mannerly girl, Master Thorney, though but a homely man's daughter; there have worse faces looked out of black bags, man.

O. Thor. You speak your mind freely and honestly. I marvel my son comes not; I am sure he will be here some time to-day.

Car. To-day or to-morrow, when he comes he shall be welcome to bread, beer, and beef, yeoman's fare; we have no kickshaws: full dishes, whole bellyfuls. Should I diet three days at one of the slender city-suppers, you might send me to Barber-Surgeons' hall the fourth day, to hang up for an anatomy.[5]—Here come they that—

[5]Skeleton.

Enter WARBECK *with* SUSAN, SOMERTON *with* KATHERINE.

How now, girls! every day play-day with you? Valentine's day too, all by couples? Thus will young folks do when we are laid in our graves, Master Thorney; here's all the care they take. And how do you find the wenches, gentlemen? have they any mind to a loose gown and a strait shoe? Win 'em and wear 'em; they shall choose for themselves by my consent.

War. You speak like a kind father.—Sue, thou hear'st
The liberty that's granted thee; what say'st thou?
Wilt thou be mine?

Sus. Your what, sir? I dare swear
Never your wife.

War. Canst thou be so unkind,
Considering how dearly I affect thee,
Nay, dote on thy perfections?

Sus. You are studied,
Too scholar-like, in words I understand not.
I am too coarse for such a gallant's love
As you are.

War. By the honour of gentility,—

Sus. Good sir, no swearing; yea and nay with us
Prevail above all oaths you can invent.

War. By this white hand of thine,—

Sus. Take a false oath!
Fie, fie! flatter the wise; fools not regard it,
And one of these am I.

War. Dost thou despise me?

Car. Let 'em talk on, Master Thorney; I know Sue's mind. The fly may buzz about the candle, he shall but singe his wings when all's done; Frank, Frank is he has her heart.

Som. But shall I live in hope, Kate?

Kath. Better so
Than be a desperate man.

Som. Perhaps thou think'st it is thy portion
I level at: wert thou as poor in fortunes
As thou art rich in goodness, I would rather
Be suitor for the dower of thy virtues
Than twice thy father's whole estate; and, prithee,
Be thou resolved[6] so.

Kath. Master Somerton,
It is an easy labour to deceive
A maid that will believe men's subtle promises;
Yet I conceive of you as worthily
As I presume you to deserve.

Som. Which is,
As worthily in loving thee sincerely
As thou art worthy to be so beloved.

Kath. I shall find time to try you.

Som. Do, Kate, do;
And when I fail, may all my joys forsake me!

Car. Warbeck and Sue are at it still. I laugh to myself, Master Thorney, to see how earnestly he beats the bush, while the bird is flown into another's bosom. A very unthrift, Master Thorney; one of the country roaring-lads: we have such as well as the city, and as arrant rake-hells as they are, though not so nimble at their prizes of wit. Sue knows the rascal to an hair's-breadth, and will fit him accordingly.

O. Thor. What is the other gentleman?

Car. One Somerton; the honester man of the two by five pound in every stone-weight. A civil fellow; he has a fine convenient estate of land in West Ham, by Essex: Master Ranges, that dwells by Enfield, sent him hither. He likes Kate well; I may tell you I think she likes him as well: if they agree, I'll not hinder the match for my part. But that Warbeck is such another—I use him kindly for Master Somerton's sake; for he came hither first as a companion of his: honest men, Master Thorney, may fall into knaves' company now and then.

War. Three hundred a-year jointure, Sue.

Sus. Where lies it?
By sea or by land? I think by sea.

[6]Persuaded.

War. Do I look like a captain?

Sus. Not a whit, sir.
Should all that use the seas be reckoned captains,
There's not a ship should have a scullion in her
To keep her clean.

War. Do you scorn me, Mistress Susan?
Am I a subject to be jeered at?

Sus. Neither
Am I a property for you to use
As stale[7] to your fond wanton loose discourse:
Pray, sir, be civil.

War. Wilt be angry, wasp?

Car. God-a-mercy, Sue! she'll firk him, on my life, if he fumble with her.

Enter FRANK.

Master Francis Thorney, you are welcome indeed; your father expected your coming. How does the right worshipful knight, Sir Arthur Clarington, your master?

Frank. In health this morning.—Sir, my duty.

O. Thor. Now
You come as I could wish.

War. [*Aside*] Frank Thorney, ha!

Sus. You must excuse me.

Frank. Virtuous Mistress Susan,
Kind Mistress Katharine. [*Kisses them.*]—Gentlemen, to both
Good time o' th' day.

Som. The like to you.

War. 'Tis he.
A word, friend. [*Aside to Som.*] On my life, this is the man
Stands fair in crossing Susan's love to me.

Som. [*Aside to War.*] I think no less; be wise, and take no notice on't;

[7]A stalking-horse, cover.

He that can win her best deserves her.

War. [*Aside to Som.*] Marry
A serving-man? mew!

Som. [*Aside to War.*] Prithee, friend, no more.

Car. Gentlemen all, there's within a slight dinner ready, if you please to taste of it; Master Thorney, Master Francis, Master Somerton.—Why, girls! what huswives! will you spend all your forenoon in tittle-tattles? away! it's well, i'faith.—Will you go in, gentlemen?

O. Thor. We'll follow presently; my son and I
Have a few words of business.

Car. At your pleasure. [*Exeunt all but* O. THOR. *and* FRANK.

O. Thor. I think you guess the reason, Frank, for which
I sent for you.

Frank. Yes, sir.

O. Thor. I need not tell you
With what a labyrinth of dangers daily
The best part of my whole estate's encumbered;
Nor have I any clue to wind it out
But what occasion proffers me; wherein
If you should falter, I shall have the shame,
And you the loss. On these two points rely
Our happiness or ruin. If you marry
With wealthy Carter's daughter, there's a portion
Will free my land; all which I will instate,[8]
Upon the marriage, to you: otherwise
I must be of necessity enforced
To make a present sale of all; and yet,
For aught I know, live in as poor distress,
Or worse, than now I do. You hear the sum?
I told you thus before; have you considered on't?

Frank. I have, sir; and however I could wish
To enjoy the benefit of single freedom,—
For that I find no disposition in me
To undergo the burthen of that care
That marriage brings with it,—yet, to secure

[8]Make over.

And settle the continuance of your credit,
I humbly yield to be directed by you
In all commands.

O. Thor. You have already used
Such thriving protestations to the maid
That she is wholly yours; and—speak the truth—
You love her, do you not?

Frank. 'Twere pity, sir,
I should deceive her.

O. Thor. Better you'd been unborn.
But is your love so steady that you mean,
Nay, more, desire, to make her your wife?

Frank. Else, sir,
It were a wrong not to be righted.

O. Thor. True,
It were: and you will marry her?

Frank. Heaven prosper it,
I do intend it.

O. Thor. O, thou art a villain!
A devil like a man! Wherein have I
Offended all the powers so much, to be
Father to such a graceless, godless son?

Frank. To me, sir, this! O, my cleft heart!

O. Thor. To thee,
Son of my curse. Speak truth and blush, thou monster!
Hast thou not married Winnifred, a maid
Was fellow-servant with thee?

Frank [*Aside*]. Some swift spirit
Has blown this news abroad; I must outface it.

O. Thor. D' you study for excuse? why, all the country
Is full on't.

Frank. With your licence, 'tis not charitable,
I'm sure it is not fatherly, so much
To be o'erswayed with credulous conceit

Of mere impossibilities; but fathers
Are privileged to think and talk at pleasure.

O. Thor. Why, canst thou yet deny thou hast no wife?

Frank. What do you take me for? an atheist?
One that nor hopes the blessedness of life
Hereafter, neither fears the vengeance due
To such as make the marriage-bed an inn,
Which travellers, day and night,
After a toilsome lodging, leave at pleasure?
Am I become so insensible of losing
The glory of creation's work, my soul?
O, I have lived too long!

O. Thor. Thou hast, dissembler.
Dar'st thou persever yet, and pull down wrath
As hot as flames of hell to strike thee quick
Into the grave of horror? I believe thee not;
Get from my sight!

Frank. Sir, though mine innocence
Needs not a stronger witness than the clearness
Of an unperished conscience, yet for that
I was informed how mainly you had been
Possessed of this untruth,—to quit all scruple,
Please you peruse this letter; 'tis to you.

O. Thor. From whom?

Frank. Sir Arthur Clarington, my master.

O. Thor. Well, sir. [*Reads.*

Frank [*Aside*]. On every side I am distracted;
Am waded deeper into mischief
Than virtue can avoid; but on I must:
Fate leads me; I will follow.—There you read
What may confirm you.

O. Thor. Yes, and wonder at it.
Forgive me, Frank; credulity abused me.
My tears express my joy; and I am sorry
I injured innocence.

Frank. Alas! I knew

Your rage and grief proceeded from your love
To me; so I conceived it.

O. Thor. My good son,
I'll bear with many faults in thee hereafter;
Bear thou with mine.

Frank. The peace is soon concluded.

Re-enter CARTER *and* SUSAN.

Car. Why, Master Thorney, d'ye mean to talk out your dinner? the company attends your coming. What must it be, Master Frank? or son Frank? I am plain Dunstable.[9]

O. Thor. Son, brother, if your daughter like to have it so.

Frank. I dare be confident she is not altered
From what I left her at our parting last:—
Are you, fair maid?

Sus. You took too sure possession
Of an engagèd heart.

Frank. Which now I challenge.

Car. Marry, and much good may it do thee, son.
Take her to thee; get me a brace of boys at a burthen,
Frank; the nursing shall not stand thee in a pennyworth
of milk; reach her home and spare not: when's
the day?

O. Thor. To-morrow, if you please. To use ceremony
Of charge and custom were to little purpose;
Their loves are married fast enough already.

Car. A good motion. We'll e'en have an household dinner, and let the fiddlers go scrape: let the bride and bridegroom dance at night together; no matter for the guests:—to-morrow, Sue, to-morrow.—Shall's to dinner now?

O. Thor. We are on all sides pleased, I hope.

Sus. Pray Heaven I may deserve the blessing sent me:
Now my heart is settled.

---

[9] *i.e.* Blunt and honest. An old proverb.

Frank. So is mine.

Car. Your marriage-money shall be received before your wedding-shoes can be pulled on. Blessing on you both!

Frank [*Aside*]. No man can hide his shame from Heaven that views him;
In vain he flees whose destiny pursues him. [*Exeunt.*

ACT THE SECOND.

SCENE I.—*The Fields near Edmonton.*

Enter MOTHER SAWYER *gathering sticks.*

MOTHER SAWYER. And why on me? why should the envious world
Throw all their scandalous malice upon me?
'Cause I am poor, deformed, and ignorant,
And like a bow buckled and bent together
By some more strong in mischiefs than myself,
Must I for that be made a common sink
For all the filth and rubbish of men's tongues
To fall and run into? Some call me witch,
And being ignorant of myself, they go
About to teach me how to be one; urging
That my bad tongue—by their bad usage made so—
Forspeaks[10] their cattle, doth bewitch their corn,
Themselves, their servants, and their babes at nurse.
This they enforce upon me, and in part
Make me to credit it; and here comes one
Of my chief adversaries.

Enter OLD BANKS.

O. Banks. Out, out upon thee, witch!

M. Saw. Dost call me witch?

O. Banks. I do, witch, I do; and worse I would, knew I a name more hateful. What makest thou upon my ground?

M. Saw. Gather a few rotten sticks to warm me.

O. Banks. Down with them when I bid thee quickly; I'll make thy bones rattle in thy skin else.

M. Saw. You won't, churl, cut-throat, miser!—there they be [*Throws them down*]: would they stuck cross thy throat, thy bowels, thy maw, thy midriff!

O. Banks. Sayest thou me so, hag? Out of my ground! [*Beats her.*

[10]Another term for "bewitch" commonly in use; the word probably implied the muttering or "forspeaking" of a spell.

M. Saw. Dost strike me, slave, curmudgeon! Now, thy bones ache, thy joints cramp, and convulsions stretch and crack thy sinews!

O. Banks. Cursing, thou hag! take that and that. [*Beats her and exit.*

M. Saw. Strike, do!—and withered may that hand and arm
Whose blows have lamed me drop from the rotten trunk.
Abuse me! beat me! call me hag and witch!
What is the name, where and by what art learned,
What spells, what charms, or invocations,
May the thing called Familiar be purchased?

Enter CUDDY BANKS *and several other Clowns.*

Cud. A new head for the tabor, and silver tipping for the pipe; remember that: and forget not five leash of new bells.

1st Cl. Double bells;—Crooked Lane[11]—ye shall have 'em straight in Crooked Lane:—double bells all, if it be possible.

Cud. Double bells? double coxcombs! trebles, buy me trebles, all trebles; for our purpose is to be in the altitudes.

2nd Cl. All trebles? not a mean?[12]

Cud. Not one. The morris is so cast, we'll have neither mean nor base in our company, fellow Rowland.

3rd Cl. What! nor a counter?[13]

Cud. By no means, no hunting counter;[14] leave that to Enfield Chase men: all trebles, all in the altitudes. Now for the disposing of parts in the morris, little or no labour will serve.

2nd Cl. If you that be minded to follow your leader know me—an ancient honour belonging to our house—for a fore-horse i' th' team and fore-gallant[15] in a morris, my father's stable is not unfurnished.

---

[11]A winding thoroughfare which led from Eastcheap to Fish-street-hill.

[12]"An inner part between the tenor and the base." *Blount's Glossographia*, 1681. It was customary in the morris to adorn the dresses of the dancers, the trappings of the hobby-horse, &c., with bells of different pitch, but arranged to sound in harmony. Hence, "treble," "mean," &c.

[13]Counter-tenor.

[14]Coursing the hare.

3rd Cl. So much for the fore-horse; but how for a good hobby-horse?

Cud. For a hobby-horse? let me see an almanac. Midsummer-moon, let me see ye. "When the moon's in the full, then's wit in the wane." No more. Use your best skill; your morris will suffer an eclipse.

1st Cl. An eclipse?

Cud. A strange one.

2nd Cl. Strange?

Cud. Yes, and most sudden. Remember the fore-gallant, and forget the hobby-horse! The whole body of your morris will be darkened.—There be of us—but 'tis no matter:—forget the hobby-horse!

1st Cl. Cuddy Banks!—have you forgot since he paced it from Enfield Chase to Edmonton?—Cuddy, honest Cuddy, cast thy stuff.

Cud. Suffer may ye all! it shall be known, I can take mine ease as well as another man. Seek your hobby-horse where you can get him.[16]

1st Cl. Cuddy, honest Cuddy, we confess, and are sorry for our neglect.

2nd Cl. The old horse shall have a new bridle.

3rd Cl. The caparisons new painted.

4th Cl. The tail repaired. The snaffle and the bosses new saffroned o'er.

1st Cl. Kind,—

2nd Cl. Honest,—

3rd Cl. Loving, ingenious,—

4th Cl. Affable Cuddy.

Cud. To show I am not flint, but affable, as you say, very well stuffed, a kind of warm dough or puff-paste, I relent, I connive, most affable Jack. Let the hobby-horse provide a strong back, he shall not want a belly when I am in him—but [*Seeing Sawyer*]—'uds me, Mother

[15]The fore-man or fore-gallant of the morris led the other dancers, and was distinguished by a gayer dress.

[16]Cuddy's anger arises from the unlucky question asked by the third clown; "How shall we do for a good hobby-horse?"—as he apparently expected, from his former celebrity in that respectable character, to have been appointed by acclamation.—*Gifford.*

Sawyer!

1st Cl. The old Witch of Edmonton!—if our mirth be not crossed—

2nd Cl. Bless us, Cuddy, and let her curse her t'other eye out.—What dost now?

Cud. "Ungirt, unblest," says the proverb; but my girdle shall serve for a riding knot; and a fig for all the witches in Christendom!—What wouldst thou?

1st Cl. The devil cannot abide to be crossed.

2nd Cl. And scorns to come at any man's whistle.

3rd Cl. Away—

4th Cl. With the witch!

All. Away with the Witch of Edmonton! [*Exeunt in strange postures.*

M. Saw. Still vexed! still tortured! that curmudgeon Banks
Is ground of all my scandal; I am shunned
And hated like a sickness; made a scorn
To all degrees and sexes. I have heard old beldams
Talk of familiars in the shape of mice,
Rats, ferrets, weasels, and I wot not what,
That have appeared, and sucked, some say, their blood;
But by what means they came acquainted with them
I am now ignorant. Would some power, good or bad,
Instruct me which way I might be revenged
Upon this churl, I'd go out of myself,
And give this fury leave to dwell within
This ruined cottage ready to fall with age,
Abjure all goodness, be at hate with prayer,
And study curses, imprecations,
Blasphemous speeches, oaths, detested oaths,
Or anything that's ill: so I might work
Revenge upon this miser, this black cur,
That barks and bites, and sucks the very blood
Of me and of my credit. 'Tis all one
To be a witch as to be counted one:
Vengeance, shame, ruin light upon that canker!

Enter a Black Dog.

Dog. Ho! have I found thee cursing? now thou art
Mine own.

M. Saw. Thine! what art thou?

Dog. He thou hast so often
Importuned to appear to thee, the devil.

M. Saw. Bless me! the devil?

Dog. Come, do not fear; I love thee much too well
To hurt or fright thee; if I seem terrible,
It is to such as hate me. I have found
Thy love unfeigned; have seen and pitied
Thy open wrongs; and come, out of my love,
To give thee just revenge against thy foes.

M. Saw. May I believe thee?

Dog. To confirm't, command me
Do any mischief unto man or beast,
And I'll effect it, on condition
That, uncompelled, thou make a deed of gift
Of soul and body to me.

M. Saw. Out, alas!
My soul and body?

Dog. And that instantly,
And seal it with thy blood: if thou deniest,
I'll tear thy body in a thousand pieces.

M. Saw. I know not where to seek relief: but shall I,
After such covenants sealed, see full revenge
On all that wrong me?

Dog. Ha, ha! silly woman!
The devil is no liar to such as he loves:
Didst ever know or hear the devil a liar
To such as he affects?

M. Saw. Then I am thine; at least so much of me
As I can call mine own—

Dog. Equivocations?
Art mine or no? speak, or I'll tear—

M. Saw. All thine.

Dog. Seal't with thy blood.

[*She pricks her arm, which he sucks. Thunder and lightning.*

See! now I dare call thee mine!
For proof, command me; instantly I'll run
To any mischief; goodness can I none.

M. Saw. And I desire as little. There's an old churl,
One Banks—

Dog. That wronged thee, lamed thee, called thee witch.

M. Saw. The same; first upon him I'd be revenged.

Dog. Thou shalt; do but name how.

M. Saw. Go, touch his life.

Dog. I cannot.

M. Saw. Hast thou not vowed? Go, kill the slave!

Dog. I wonnot.

M. Saw. I'll cancel, then, my gift.

Dog. Ha, ha!

M. Saw. Dost laugh!
Why wilt not kill him?

Dog. Fool, because I cannot.
Though we have power, know it is circumscribed
And tied in limits: though he be curst to thee,
Yet of himself he's loving to the world,
And charitable to the poor: now men that,
As he, love goodness, though in smallest measure,
Live without compass of our reach. His cattle
And corn I'll kill and mildew; but his life—
Until I take him, as I late found thee,
Cursing and swearing—I've no power to touch.

M. Saw. Work on his corn and cattle, then.

Dog. I shall.

The Witch of Edmonton shall see his fall;
If she at least put credit in my power,
And in mine only; make orisons to me,
And none but me.

M. Saw. Say how and in what manner.

Dog. I'll tell thee: when thou wishest ill,
Corn, man, or beast wouldst spoil or kill,
Turn thy back against the sun,
And mumble this short orison:
"If thou to death or shame pursue 'em,
Sanctibicetur nomen tuum."

M. Saw. "If thou to death or shame pursue 'em,
Sanctibicetur nomen tuum."

Dog. Perfect: farewell. Our first-made promises
We'll put in execution against Banks. [*Exit.*

M. Saw. Contaminetur nomen tuum. I'm an expert scholar;
Speak Latin, or I know not well what language,
As well as the best of 'em—but who comes here?

Re-enter CUDDY BANKS.

The son of my worst foe.

To death pursue 'em,
Et sanctibicetur nomen tuum.

Cud. What's that she mumbles? the devil's paternoster? would it were else!—Mother Sawyer, good-morrow.

M. Saw. Ill-morrow to thee, and all the world that flout
A poor old woman,

To death pursue 'em,
And *sanctibicetur nomen tuum.*

Cud. Nay, good Gammer Sawyer, whate'er it pleases my father to call you, I know you are—

M. Saw. A witch.

Cud. A witch? would you were else i'faith!

M. Saw. Your father knows I am by this.

Cud. I would he did.

M. Saw. And so in time may you.

Cud. I would I might else! But, witch or no witch, you are a motherly woman; and though my father be a kind of God-bless-us, as they say, I have an earnest suit to you; and if you'll be so kind to ka me one good turn, I'll be so courteous as to kob[17] you another.

M. Saw. What's that? to spurn, beat me, and call me witch,
As your kind father doth?

Cud. My father! I am ashamed to own him. If he has hurt the head of thy credit, there's money to buy thee a plaster [*Gives her money*]; and a small courtesy I would require at thy hands.

M. Saw. You seem a good young man, and—[*Aside*] I must dissemble,
The better to accomplish my revenge.—
But—for this silver, what wouldst have me do?
Bewitch thee?

Cud. No, by no means; I am bewitched already: I would have thee so good as to unwitch me, or witch another with me for company.

M. Saw. I understand thee not; be plain, my son.

Cud. As a pike-staff, mother. You know Kate Carter?

M. Saw. The wealthy yeoman's daughter? what of her?

Cud. That same party has bewitched me.

M. Saw. Bewitched thee?

Cud. Bewitched me, *hisce auribus*. I saw a little devil fly out of her eye like a burbolt,[18] which sticks at this hour up to the feathers in my heart. Now, my request is, to send one of thy what-d'ye-call-'ems either to pluck that out, or stick another as fast in hers: do, and here's my hand, I am thine for three lives.

M. Saw. [*Aside*] We shall have sport.—Thou art in love with her?

---

[17]"Ka me, ka thee!" was an old proverb.

[18]Bird-bolt, arrow; perhaps more correctly "But-bolt," as emendated by Gifford.

Cud. Up to the very hilts, mother.

M. Saw. And thou wouldst have me make her love thee too?

Cud. [*Aside*] I think she'll prove a witch in earnest.—Yes, I could find in my heart to strike her three quarters deep in love with me too.

M. Saw. But dost thou think that I can do't, and I alone?

Cud. Truly, Mother Witch, I do verily believe so; and, when I see it done, I shall be half persuaded so too.

M. Saw. It is enough: what art can do be sure of.
Turn to the west, and whatsoe'er thou hear'st
Or seest, stand silent, and be not afraid.

[*She stamps on the ground; the Dog appears, and fawns, and leaps upon her.*

Cud. Afraid, Mother Witch!—"turn my face to the west!" I said I should always have a back-friend of her; and now it's out. An her little devil should be hungry, come sneaking behind me, like a cowardly catchpole, and clap his talons on my haunches—'Tis woundy cold, sure—I dudder and shake like an aspen-leaf every joint of me.

M. Saw. To scandal and disgrace pursue 'em,
Et sanctibicetur nomen tuum. [*Exit Dog.*

How now, my son, how is't?

Cud. Scarce in a clean life, Mother Witch.—But did your goblin and you spout Latin together?

M. Saw. A kind of charm I work by; didst thou hear me?

Cud. I heard I know not the devil what mumble in a scurvy base tone, like a drum that had taken cold in the head the last muster. Very comfortable words; what were they? and who taught them you?

M. Saw. A great learned man.

Cud. Learned man! learned devil it was as soon! But what? what comfortable news about the party?

M. Saw. Who? Kate Carter? I'll tell thee. Thou knowest the stile at the west end of thy father's peas-field: be there to-morrow night after sunset; and the first live thing thou seest be sure to follow, and that shall bring thee to thy love.

Cud. In the peas-field? has she a mind to codlings[19] already? The first living thing I meet, you say, shall bring me to her?

M. Saw. To a sight of her, I mean. She will seem wantonly coy, and flee thee; but follow her close and boldly: do but embrace her in thy arms once, and she is thine own.

Cud. "At the stile at the west end of my father's peas-land, the first live thing I see, follow and embrace her, and she shall be thine." Nay, an I come to embracing once, she shall be mine; I'll go near to make at eaglet else. [*Exit.*

M. Saw. A ball well bandied! now the set's half won;
The father's wrong I'll wreak upon the son. [*Exit.*

SCENE II.—Carter's *House.*

Enter Carter, Warbeck, *and* Somerton.

Car. How now, gentlemen! cloudy? I know, Master Warbeck, you are in a fog about my daughter's marriage.

War. And can you blame me, sir?

Car. Nor you me justly. Wedding and hanging are tied up both in a proverb; and destiny is the juggler that unties the knot. My hope is, you are reserved to a richer fortune than my poor daughter.

War. However, your promise—

Car. Is a kind of debt, I confess it.

War. Which honest men should pay.

Car. Yet some gentlemen break in that point now and then, by your leave, sir.

Som. I confess thou hast had a little wrong in the wench; but patience is the only salve to cure it. Since Thorney has won the wench, he has most reason to wear her.

War. Love in this kind admits no reason to wear her.

---

[19]Peas codlings; green peas.

Car. Then Love's a fool, and what wise man will take exception?

Som. Come, frolic, Ned: were every man master of his own fortune, Fate might pick straws, and Destiny go a-wool-gathering.

War. You hold yours in a string, though: 'tis well; but if there be any equity, look thou to meet the like usage ere long.

Som. In my love to her sister Katherine? Indeed, they are a pair of arrows drawn out of one quiver, and should fly at an even length; if she do run after her sister.—

War. Look for the same mercy at my hands as I have received at thine.

Som. She'll keep a surer compass; I have too strong a confidence to mistrust her.

War. And that confidence is a wind that has blown many a married man ashore at Cuckold's Haven, I can tell you; I wish yours more prosperous though.

Car. Whate'er your wish, I'll master my promise to him.

War. Yes, as you did to me.

Car. No more of that, if you love me: but for the more assurance, the next offered occasion shall consummate the marriage; and that once sealed—

Som. Leave the manage of the rest to my care. But see, the bridegroom and bride come; the new pair of Sheffield knives, fitted both to one sheath.

War. The sheath might have been better fitted, if somebody had their due; but—

Car. No harsh language, if thou lovest me. Frank Thorney has done—

War. No more than I, or thou, or any man, things so standing, would have attempted.

Enter Frank Thorney *and* Susan.

Som. Good-morrow, Master Bridegroom.

War. Come, give thee joy: mayst thou live long and happy
In thy fair choice!

Frank. I thank ye, gentlemen; kind Master Warbeck,
I find you loving.

War. Thorney, that creature,—much good do thee with her!—
Virtue and beauty hold fair mixture in her;
She's rich, no doubt, in both: yet were she fairer,
Thou art right worthy of her. Love her, Thorney;
'Tis nobleness in thee, in her but duty.
The match is fair and equal; the success
I leave to censure. Farewell, Mistress Bride!
Till now elected, thy old scorn deride. [*Exit.*

Som. Good Master Thorney—

Car. Nay, you shall not part till you see the barrels run a-tilt, gentlemen. [*Exit with* SOMERTON.

Sus. Why change you your face, sweetheart?

Frank. Who, I? for nothing.

Sus. Dear, say not so; a spirit of your constancy
Cannot endure this change for nothing.
I have observed strange variations in you.

Frank. In me?

Sus. In you, sir.
Awake, you seem to dream, and in your sleep
You utter sudden and distracted accents,
Like one at enmity with peace. Dear loving husband,
If I
May dare to challenge any interest in you,
Give me the reason fully; you may trust
My breast as safely as your own.

Frank. With what?
You half amaze me; prithee—

Sus. Come, you shall not,
Indeed you shall not, shut me from partaking
The least dislike that grieves you; I'm all yours.

Frank. And I all thine.

Sus. You are not, if you keep

The least grief from me: but I find the cause;
It grew from me.

Frank. From you?

Sus. From some distaste
In me or my behaviour: you're not kind
In the concealment. 'Las, sir, I am young,
Silly and plain; more, strange to those contents
A wife should offer: say but in what I fail,
I'll study satisfaction.

Frank. Come; in nothing.

Sus. I know I do; knew I as well in what,
You should not long be sullen. Prithee, love,
If I have been immodest or too bold,
Speak't in a frown; if peevishly too nice,
Show't in a smile: thy liking is the glass
By which I'll habit my behaviour.

Frank. Wherefore dost weep now?

Sus. You, sweet, have the power
To make me passionate as an April-day;
Now smile, then weep; now pale, then crimson red:
You are the powerful moon of my blood's sea,
To make it ebb or flow into my face,
As your looks change.

Frank. Change thy conceit, I prithee;
Thou art all perfection: Diana herself
Swells in thy thoughts and moderates thy beauty.
Within thy left eye amorous Cupid sits,
Feathering love-shafts, whose golden heads he dipped
In[20] thy chaste breast; in the other lies
Blushing Adonis scarfed in modesties;
And still as wanton Cupid blows love-fires,
Adonis quenches out unchaste desires;
And from these two I briefly do imply
A perfect emblem of thy modesty.
Then, prithee, dear, maintain no more dispute,
For when thou speak'st, it's fit all tongues be mute.

[20]There is a break here in the quarto. It is suggested that the printer was unable to decipher the first word of the line in the manuscript.

Sus. Come, come, these golden strings of flattery
Shall not tie up my speech, sir; I must know
The ground of your disturbance.

Frank. Then look here;
For here, here is the fen in which this hydra
Of discontent grows rank.

Sus. Heaven shield it! where?

Frank. In mine own bosom, here the cause has root;
The poisoned leeches twist about my heart,
And will, I hope, confound me.

Sus. You speak riddles.

Frank. Take't plainly, then: 'twas told me by a woman
Known and approved in palmistry,
I should have two wives.

Sus. Two wives? sir, I take it
Exceeding likely; but let not conceit hurt you:
You're afraid to bury me?

Frank. No, no, my Winnifred.

Sus. How say you? Winnifred! you forget me.

Frank. No, I forget myself!—Susan.

Sus. In what?

Frank. Talking of wives, I pretend Winnifred,
A maid that at my mother's waited on me
Before thyself.

Sus. I hope, sir, she may live
To take my place: but why should all this move you?

Frank. The poor girl!—[*Aside.*] she has't before thee,
And that's the fiend torments me.

Sus. Yet why should this
Raise mutiny within you? such presages
Prove often false: or say it should be true?

Frank. That I should have another wife?

Sus. Yes, many;
If they be good, the better.

Frank. Never any
Equal to thee in goodness.

Sus. Sir, I could wish I were much better for you;
Yet if I knew your fate
Ordained you for another, I could wish—
So well I love you and your hopeful pleasure—
Me in my grave, and my poor virtues added
To my successor.

Frank. Prithee, prithee, talk not
Of deaths or graves; thou art so rare a goodness
As Death would rather put itself to death
Than murder thee: but we, as all things else,
Are mutable and changing.

Sus. Yet you still move
In your first sphere of discontent. Sweet, chase
Those clouds of sorrow, and shine clearly on me.

Frank. At my return I will.

Sus. Return! ah me!
Will you, then, leave me?

Frank. For a time I must:
But how? As birds their young, or loving bees
Their hives, to fetch home richer dainties.

Sus. Leave me!
Now has my fear met its effect. You shall not;
Cost it my life, you shall not.

Frank. Why? your reason?

Sus. Like to the lapwing have you all this while
With your false love deluded me, pretending
Counterfeit senses for your discontent;
And now at last it is by chance stole from you.

Frank. What? what by chance?

Sus. Your pre-appointed meeting

Of single combat with young Warbeck.

Frank. Ha!

Sus. Even so: dissemble not; 'tis too apparent:
Then in his look I read it:—deny it not,
I see't apparent; cost it my undoing,
And unto that my life, I will not leave you.

Frank. Not until when?

Sus. Till he and you be friends.
Was this your cunning?—and then flam me off
With an old witch, two wives, and Winnifred!
You're not so kind, indeed, as I imagined.

Frank. [*Aside.*] And you are more fond by far than I expected.—
It is a virtue that attends thy kind—
But of our business within: and by this kiss,
I'll anger thee no more; 'troth, chuck, I will not.

Sus. You shall have no just cause.

Frank. Dear Sue, I shall not. [*Exeunt.*

ACT THE THIRD.

SCENE I.—*The Village Green.*

Enter CUDDY BANKS *with the Morris-dancers.*

FIRST CLOWN. Nay, Cuddy, prithee do not leave us now; if we part all this night, we shall not meet before day.

2nd Cl. I prithee, Banks, let's keep together now.

Cud. If you were wise, a word would serve; but as you are, I must be forced to tell you again, I have a little private business, an hour's work; it may prove but an half hour's, as luck may serve; and then I take horse, and along with you. Have we e'er a witch in the morris?

1st Cl. No, no; no woman's part but Maid Marian and the Hobby-horse.

Cud. I'll have a witch; I love a witch.

1st Cl. 'Faith, witches themselves are so common now-a-days, that the counterfeit will not be regarded. They say we have three or four in Edmonton besides Mother Sawyer.

2nd Cl. I would she would dance her part with us.

3rd Cl. So would not I; for if she comes, the devil and all comes along with her.

Cud. Well, I'll have a witch; I have loved a witch ever since I played at cherry-pit.[21] Leave me, and get my horse dressed; give him oats: but water him not till I come. Whither do we foot it first?

2nd Cl. To Sir Arthur Clarington's first; then whither thou wilt.

Cud. Well, I am content; but we must up to Carter's, the rich yeoman; I must be seen on hobby-horse there.

1st Cl. O, I smell him now!—I'll lay my ears Banks is in love, and that's the reason he would walk melancholy by himself.

Cud. Ha! who was that said I was in love?

---

[21]A children's game, in which cherry-stones are pitched into a small hole. The suggestion was sometimes a less innocent one, however. Compare Herrick's quatrain on "Cherry-pit."

1st Cl. Not I.

2nd Cl. Nor I.

Cud. Go to, no more of that: when I understand what you speak, I know what you say; believe that.

1st Cl. Well, 'twas I, I'll not deny it; I meant no hurt in't. I have seen you walk up to Carter's of Chessum: Banks, were not you there last Shrovetide?

Cud. Yes, I was ten days together there the last Shrovetide.

2nd Cl. How could that be, when there are but seven days in the week?

Cud. Prithee peace! I reckon *stila nova* as a traveller; thou understandest as a fresh-water farmer, that never sawest a week beyond sea. Ask any soldier that ever received his pay but in the Low Countries, and he'll tell thee there are eight days in the week[22] there hard by. How dost thou think they rise in High Germany, Italy, and those remoter places?

3rd Cl. Ay, but simply there are but seven days in the week yet.

Cud. No, simply as thou understandest. Prithee look but in the lover's almanac: when he has been but three days absent, "O," says he, "I have not seen my love these seven years:" there's a long cut! When he comes to her again and embraces her, "O," says he, "now methinks I am in Heaven;" and that's a pretty step! He that can get up to Heaven in ten days need not repent his journey; you may ride a hundred days in a caroche,[23] and be further off than when you set forth. But, I pray you, good morris-mates, now leave me. I will be with you by midnight.

1st Cl. Well, since he will be alone, we'll back again and trouble him no more.

All the Clowns. But remember, Banks.

Cud. The hobby-horse shall be remembered. But hark you; get Poldavis, the barber's boy, for the witch, because he can show his art better than another. [*Exeunt all but* CUDDY.

[22]Thus Butler:

"The soldier does it every day,
Eight to the week, for sixpence pay."—*Gifford.*

[23]Coach, Fr. *Carrosse.*

Well, now to my walk. I am near the place where I should meet—I know not what: say I meet a thief? I must follow him, if to the gallows; say I meet a horse, or hare, or hound? still I must follow: some slow-paced beast, I hope; yet love is full of lightness in the heaviest lovers. Ha! my guide is come.

Enter the Dog.

A water-dog! I am thy first man, sculler; I go with thee; ply no other but myself. Away with the boat! land me but at Katherine's Dock, my sweet Katherine's Dock, and I'll be a fare to thee. That way? nay, which way thou wilt; thou knowest the way better than I:—fine gentle cur it is, and well brought up, I warrant him. We go a-ducking, spaniel; thou shalt fetch me the ducks, pretty kind rascal.

Enter a Spirit vizarded. He throws off his mask, &c., and appears in the shape of KATHERINE.

Spir. Thus throw I off mine own essential horror,
And take the shape of a sweet lovely maid
Whom this fool dotes on: we can meet his folly,
But from his virtues must be runaways.
We'll sport with him; but when we reckoning call,
We know where to receive; the witch pays for all. [*The Dog barks.*

Cud. Ay? is that the watchword? She's come. [*Sees the Spirit.*] Well, if ever we be married, it shall be at Barking Church,[24] in memory of thee: now come behind, kind cur.

And have I met thee, sweet Kate?
I will teach thee to walk so late.

O, see, we meet in metre. [*The Spirit retires as he advances.*] What! dost thou trip from me? O, that I were upon my hobby-horse, I would mount after thee so nimble! "Stay, nymph, stay, nymph," singed Apollo.

Tarry and kiss me, sweet nymph, stay;
Tarry and kiss me, sweet:
We will to Chessum Street,
And then to the house stands in the highway.

Nay, by your leave, I must embrace you. [*Exit, following the Spirit.*

[24]Barking Church stood at the bottom of Seething Lane. It was destroyed in the great fire.—*Gifford.*

[*Within.*] O, help, help! I am drowned, I am drowned!

Re-enter CUDDY *wet.*

Dog. Ha, ha, ha, ha!

Cud. This was an ill night to go a-wooing in; I find it now in Pond's almanac: thinking to land at Katherine's Dock, I was almost at Gravesend. I'll never go to a wench in the dog-days again; yet 'tis cool enough.—Had you never a paw in this dog-trick? a mange take that black hide of yours! I'll throw you in at Limehouse in some tanner's pit or other.

Dog. Ha, ha, ha, ha!

Cud. How now! who's that laughs at me? Hist to him! [*The Dog barks.*] —Peace, peace! thou didst but thy kind neither; 'twas my own fault.

Dog. Take heed how thou trustest the devil another time.

Cud. How now! who's that speaks? I hope you have not your reading tongue about you?

Dog. Yes, I can speak.

Cud. The devil you can! you have read Æsop's fables, then; I have played one of your parts then,—the dog that catched at the shadow in the water. Pray you, let me catechise you a little; what might one call your name, dog?

Dog. My dame calls me Tom.

Cud. 'Tis well, and she may call me Ass; so there's an whole one betwixt us, Tom-Ass: she said I should follow you, indeed. Well, Tom, give me thy fist, we are friends; you shall be mine ingle:[25] I love you; but I pray you let's have no more of these ducking devices.

Dog. Not, if you love me. Dogs love where they are beloved; cherish me, and I'll do anything for thee.

Cud. Well, you shall have jowls and livers; I have butchers to my friends that shall bestow 'em: and I will keep crusts and bones for you, if you'll be a kind dog, Tom.

Dog. Any thing; I'll help thee to thy love.

---

[25]Crony, friend.

Cud. Wilt thou? that promise shall cost me a brown loaf, though I steal it out of my father's cupboard: you'll eat stolen goods, Tom, will you not?

Dog. O, best of all; the sweetest bits those.

Cud. You shall not starve, Ningle[26] Tom, believe that: if you love fish, I'll help you to maids and soles; I'm acquainted with a fishmonger.

Dog. Maids and soles? O, sweet bits! banqueting stuff those.

Cud. One thing I would request you, ningle, as you have played the knavish cur with me a little, that you would mingle amongst our morris-dancers in the morning. You can dance?

Dog. Yes, yes, any thing; I'll be there, but unseen to any but thyself. Get thee gone before; fear not my presence. I have work to-night; I serve more masters, more dames than one.

Cud. He can serve Mammon and the devil too.

Dog. It shall concern thee and thy love's purchase.
There is a gallant rival loves the maid,
And likely is to have her. Mark what a mischief,
Before the morris ends, shall light on him!

Cud. O, sweet ningle, thy neuf[27] once again; friends must part for a time. Farewell, with this remembrance; shalt have bread too when we meet again. If ever there were an honest devil, 'twill be the Devil of Edmonton,[28] I see. Farewell, Tom; I prithee dog me as soon as thou canst. [*Exit.*

Dog. I'll not miss thee, and be merry with thee.
Those that are joys denied must take delight
In sins and mischiefs; 'tis the devil's right. [*Exit.*

SCENE II.—*The neighbourhood of Edmonton.*

Enter FRANK THORNEY *and* WINNIFRED *in boy's clothes.*

[26]Abbreviation for "Mine ingle," as above.

[27]Or "neif," *i.e.* fist.

[28]The allusion is to Master Peter Fabel, who, as the prologue to the old comedy says, "was called, for his sleights and his magic, "The merry Devil of Edmonton."—*Gifford.*

Frank. Prithee no more! those tears give nourishment
To weeds and briers in me, which shortly will
O'ergrow and top my head; my shame will sit
And cover all that can be seen of me.

Win. I have not shown this cheek in company;
Pardon me now: thus singled with yourself,
It calls a thousand sorrows round about,
Some going before, and some on either side,
But infinite behind; all chained together:
Your second adulterous marriage leads;
That is the sad eclipse, th' effects must follow,
As plagues of shame, spite, scorn, and obloquy.

Frank. Why, hast thou not left one hour's patience
To add to all the rest? one hour bears us
Beyond the reach of all these enemies:
Are we not now set forward in the flight,
Provided with the dowry of my sin[29]
To keep us in some other nation?
While we together are, we are at home
In any place.

Win. 'Tis foul ill-gotten coin,
Far worse than usury or extortion.

Frank. Let
My father, then, make the restitution,
Who forced me to take the bribe: it is his gift
And patrimony to me; so I receive it.
He would not bless, nor look a father on me,
Until I satisfied his angry will:
When I was sold, I sold myself again—
Some knaves have done't in lands, and I in body—
For money, and I have the hire. But, sweet, no more,
'Tis hazard of discovery, our discourse;
And then prevention takes off all our hopes:
For only but to take her leave of me
My wife is coming.

Win. Who coming? your wife!

Frank. No, no; thou art here: the woman—I knew

[29]Frank alludes to the marriage portion which he had just received with Susan.—*Gifford.*

Not how to call her now; but after this day
She shall be quite forgot and have no name
In my remembrance. See, see! she's come.

Enter SUSAN.

Go lead
The horses to th' hill's top; there I'll meet thee.

Sus. Nay, with your favour let him stay a little;
I would part with him too, because he is
Your sole companion; and I'll begin with him,
Reserving you the last.

Frank. Ay, with all my heart.

Sus. You may hear, if't please you, sir.

Frank. No, 'tis not fit:
Some rudiments, I conceive, they must be,
To overlook my slippery footings: and so—

Sus. No, indeed, sir.

Frank. Tush, I know it must be so,
And it is necessary: on! but be brief. [*Walks forward.*

Win. What charge soe'er you lay upon me, mistress,
I shall support it faithfully—being honest—
To my best strength.

Sus. Believe't shall be no other.
I know you were commended to my husband
By a noble knight.

Win. O, gods! O, mine eyes!

Sus. How now! what ail'st thou, lad?

Win. Something hit mine eye,—it makes it water still,—
Even as you said "commended to my husband."—
Some dor[30] I think it was.—I was, forsooth,
Commended to him by Sir Arthur Clarington.

Sus. Whose servant once my Thorney was himself.

[30]Cockchafer, beetle.

That title, methinks, should make you almost fellows;
Or at the least much more than a servant;
And I am sure he will respect you so.
Your love to him, then, needs no spur from me,
And what for my sake you will ever do,
'Tis fit it should be bought with something more
Than fair entreats; look! here's a jewel for thee,
A pretty wanton label for thine ear;
And I would have it hang there, still to whisper
These words to thee, "Thou hast my jewel with thee."
It is but earnest of a larger bounty,
When thou return'st with praises of thy service,
Which I am confident thou wilt deserve.
Why, thou art many now besides thyself:
Thou mayst be servant, friend, and wife to him;
A good wife is them all. A friend can play
The wife and servant's part, and shift enough;
No less the servant can the friend and wife:
'Tis all but sweet society, good counsel,
Interchanged loves, yes, and counsel-keeping.

Frank. Not done yet?

Sus. Even now, sir.

Win. Mistress, believe my vow; your severe eye,
Were't present to command, your bounteous hand,
Were it then by to buy or bribe my service,
Shall not make me more dear or near unto him
Than I shall voluntary. I'll be all your charge,
Servant, friend, wife to him.

Sus. Wilt thou?
Now blessings go with thee for't! courtesies
Shall meet thee coming home.

Win. Pray you say plainly,
Mistress, are you jealous of him? if you be,
I'll look to him that way too.

Sus. Say'st thou so?
I would thou hadst a woman's bosom now;
We have weak thoughts within us. Alas,
There's nothing so strong in us as suspicion;

But I dare not, nay, I will not think
So hardly of my Thorney.

Win. Believe it, mistress,
I'll be no pander to him; and if I find
Any loose lubric scapes in him, I'll watch him,
And at my return protest I'll show you all:
He shall hardly offend without my knowledge.

Sus. Thine own diligence is that I press,
And not the curious eye over his faults.
Farewell: if I should never see thee more,
Take it for ever.

Frank. Prithee take that along with thee, [*Handing his sword to* WINNIFRED.] and haste thee
To the hill's top; I'll be there instantly.

Sus. No haste, I prithee; slowly as thou canst—[*Exit* WINNIFRED.
Pray let him obey me now; 'tis happily
His last service to me: my power is e'en
A-going out of sight.

Frank. Why would you delay?
We have no other business now but to part.

Sus. And will not that, sweetheart, ask a long time?
Methinks it is the hardest piece of work
That e'er I took in hand.

Frank. Fie, fie! why, look,
I'll make it plain and easy to you—farewell! [*Kisses her.*

Sus. Ah, 'las, I'm not half perfect in it yet;
I must have it read o'er an hundred times:
Pray you take some pains; I confess my dulness.

Frank. [*Aside.*] What a thorn this rose grows on! Parting were sweet;
But what a trouble 'twill be to obtain it!—
Come, again and again, farewell!—[*Kisses her.*] Yet wilt return?
All questions of my journey, my stay, employment,
And revisitation, fully I have answered all;
There's nothing now behind but—nothing.

Sus. And
That *nothing* is more hard than anything,

Than all the everythings. This request—

Frank. What is't?

Sus. That I may bring you through one pasture more
Up to yon knot of trees; amongst those shadows
I'll vanish from you, they shall teach me how.

Frank. Why, 'tis granted; come, walk, then.

Sus. Nay, not too fast:
They say slow things have best perfection;
The gentle shower wets to fertility,
The churlish storm may mischief with his bounty;
The baser beasts take strength even from the womb,
But the lord lion's whelp is feeble long. [*Exeunt.*

SCENE III.—*A Field with a clump of trees.*

Enter the Dog.

Dog. Now for an early mischief and a sudden!
The mind's about it now; one touch from me
Soon sets the body forward.

Enter FRANK *and* SUSAN.

Frank. Your request
Is out; yet will you leave me?

Sus. What? so churlishly?
You'll make me stay for ever,
Rather than part with such a sound from you.

Frank. Why, you almost anger me. Pray you be gone.
You have no company, and 'tis very early;
Some hurt may betide you homewards.

Sus. Tush! I fear none;
To leave you is the greatest hurt I can suffer:
Besides, I expect your father and mine own
To meet me back, or overtake me with you;
They began to stir when I came after you
I know they'll not be long.

Frank. So! I shall have more trouble,—[*The Dog rubs against him*]—thank you for that:[31]
[*Aside.*] Then I'll ease all at once. It is done now;
What I ne'er thought on.—You shall not go back.

Sus. Why, shall I go along with thee? sweet music!

Frank. No, to a better place.

Sus. Any place I;
I'm there at home where thou pleasest to have me.

Frank. At home? I'll leave you in your last lodging;
I must kill you.

Sus. O, fine! you'd fright me from you.

Frank. You see I had no purpose; I'm unarmed;
'Tis this minute's decree, and it must be:
Look, this will serve your turn. [*Draws a knife.*

Sus. I'll not turn from it,
If you be earnest, sir; yet you may tell me
Wherefore you'll kill me.

Frank. Because you are a whore.

Sus. There's one deep wound already; a whore!
'Twas ever further from me than the thought
Of this black hour; a whore?

Frank. Yes, I'll prove it,
And you shall confess it. You are my whore.
No wife of mine; the word admits no second.
I was before wedded to another; have her still.
I do not lay the sin unto your charge,
'Tis all mine own: your marriage was my theft,
For I espoused your dowry, and I have it.
I did not purpose to have added murder;
The devil did not prompt me till this minute:
You might have safe returned; now you cannot.
You have dogged your own death. [*Stabs her.*

Sus. And I deserve it;

---

[31]The dog is of course supposed invisible. Frank thanks Susan for telling him of the threatened arrival of Carter and Old Thorney which would lead to discovery.

I'm glad my fate was so intelligent:
'Twas some good spirit's motion. Die? O, 'twas time!
How many years might I have slept in sin,
The sin of my most hatred, too, adultery!

Frank. Nay, sure, 'twas likely that the most was past;
For I meant never to return to you
After this parting.

Sus. Why, then, I thank you more;
You have done lovingly, leaving yourself,
That you would thus bestow me on another.
Thou art my husband, Death, and I embrace thee
With all the love I have. Forget the stain
Of my unwitting sin; and then I come
A crystal virgin to thee: my soul's purity
Shall with bold wings ascend the doors of Mercy;
For Innocence is ever her companion.

Frank. Not yet mortal? I would not linger you,
Or leave you a tongue to blab. [*Stabs her again.*

Sus. Now Heaven reward you ne'er the worse for me!
I did not think that Death had been so sweet,
Nor I so apt to love him. I could ne'er die better,
Had I stayed forty years for preparation;
For I'm in charity with all the world.
Let me for once be thine example, Heaven;
Do to this man as I him free forgive,
And may he better die and better live. [*Dies.*

Frank. 'Tis done; and I am in! Once past our height,
We scorn the deep'st abyss. This follows now,
To heal her wounds by dressing of the weapon.[32]
Arms, thighs, hands, any place; we must not fail [*Wounds himself.*
Light scratches, giving such deep ones: the best I can
To bind myself to this tree. Now's the storm,
Which if blown o'er, many fair days may follow.

[*Binds himself to a tree; the Dog ties him behind and exit.*

So, so, I'm fast; I did not think I could
Have done so well behind me. How prosperous

---

[32]An allusion to an old superstition in which the idea was that wounds were healed by the turning of the assailant's weapon against himself so as to cover it with his blood.

And effectual mischief sometimes is!—[*Aloud*] Help! help!
Murder, murder, murder!

Enter CARTER *and* OLD THORNEY.

Car. Ha! whom tolls the bell for?

Frank. O, O!

O. Thor. Ah me!
The cause appears too soon; my child, my son!

Car. Susan, girl, child! not speak to thy father? ha!

Frank. O, lend me some assistance to o'ertake
This hapless woman.

O. Thor. Let's o'ertake the murderers.
Speak whilst thou canst, anon may be too late;
I fear thou hast death's mark upon thee too.

Frank. I know them both; yet such an oath is passed
As pulls damnation up if it be broke.
I dare not name 'em: think what forced men do.

O. Thor. Keep oath with murderers! that were a conscience
To hold the devil in.

Frank. Nay, sir, I can describe 'em,
Shall show them as familiar as their names:
The taller of the two at this time wears
His satin doublet white, but crimson-lined,
Hose of black satin, cloak of scarlet—

O. Thor. Warbeck,
Warbeck, Warbeck!—do you list to this, sir?

Car. Yes, yes, I listen you; here's nothing to be heard.

Frank. Th' other's cloak branched[33] velvet, black, velvet-lined his suit.

O. Thor. I have 'em already; Somerton, Somerton!
Binal revenge all this. Come, sir, the first work
Is to pursue the murderers, when we have
Removed these mangled bodies hence.

---

[33]*i.e.* Adorned with tufts, or tassels, dependent from the shoulders.—*Gifford.*

Car. Sir, take that carcass there, and give me this.
I will not own her now; she's none of mine.
Bob me off with a dumb-show! no, I'll have life.
This is my son too, and while there's life in him,
'Tis half mine; take you half that silence for't.—
When I speak I look to be spoken to:
Forgetful slut!

O. Thor. Alas, what grief may do now!
Look, sir, I'll take this load of sorrow with me.

Car. Ay, do, and I'll have this. [*Exit* OLD THORNEY *with* SUSAN *in his arms.*] How do you, sir?

Frank. O, very ill, sir.

Car. Yes,
I think so; but 'tis well you can speak yet:
There's no music but in sound; sound it must be.
I have not wept these twenty years before,
And that I guess was ere that girl was born;
Yet now methinks, if I but knew the way,
My heart's so full, I could weep night and day. [*Exit with* FRANK.

SCENE IV.—*Before* SIR ARTHUR CLARINGTON'S *House.*

Enter SIR ARTHUR CLARINGTON, WARBECK, *and* SOMERTON.

Sir Arth. Come, gentlemen, we must all help to grace
The nimble-footed youth of Edmonton,
That are so kind to call us up to-day
With an high morris.

War. I could wish it for the best, it were the worst now. Absurdity's in my opinion ever the best dancer in a morris.

Som. I could rather sleep than see 'em.

Sir Arth. Not well, sir?

Som. 'Faith, not ever thus leaden: yet I know no cause for't.

War. Now am I beyond mine own condition highly disposed to mirth.

Sir Arth. Well, you may have yet a morris to help both;

To strike you in a dump, and make him merry.

Enter SAWGUT *with the Morris-dancers, &c.*

Saw. Come, will you set yourselves in morris-ray?[34] the forebell, second-bell, tenor, and great-bell; Maid Marian[35] for the same bell. But where's the weathercock now? the Hobby-horse?

1st Cl. Is not Banks come yet? What a spite 'tis!

Sir Arth. When set you forward, gentlemen?

1st Cl. We stay but for the Hobby-horse, sir; all our footmen are ready.

Som. 'Tis marvel your horse should be behind your foot.

2nd Cl. Yes, sir, he goes further about; we can come in at the wicket, but the broad gate must be opened for him.

Enter CUDDY BANKS *with the Hobby-horse, followed by the Dog.*

Sit Arth. O, we stayed for you, sir.

Cud. Only my horse wanted a shoe, sir; but we shall make you amends ere we part.

Sir Arth. Ay? well said; make 'em drink ere they begin.

Enter Servants with beer.

Cud. A bowl, I prithee, and a little for my horse; he'll mount the better. Nay, give me: I must drink to him, he'll not pledge else. [*Drinks.*] Here, Hobby [*Holds the bowl to the Hobby-horse.*]—I pray you: no? not drink! You see, gentlemen, we can but bring our horse to the water; he may choose whether he'll drink or no. [*Drinks again.*

Som. A good moral made plain by history.

1st Cl. Strike up, Father Sawgut, strike up.

Saw. E'en when you will, children. [CUDDY *mounts the Hobby.*]—Now in the name of—the best foot forward! [*Endeavours to play, but the fiddle gives no sound.*]—How now! not a word in thy guts? I think, children, my instrument has caught cold on the sudden.

[34]Array.

[35]Maid Marian was always a prominent figure in the morris-dance. Robin Hood, Friar Tuck, and other characters were also added according to the humour of the dancers.

Cud. [*Aside.*] My ningle's knavery; black Tom's doing.

All the Clowns. Why, what mean you, Father Sawgut?

Cud. Why, what would you have him do? you hear his fiddle is speechless.

Saw. I'll lay mine ear to my instrument that my poor fiddle is bewitched. I played "The Flowers in May" e'en now, as sweet as a violet; now 'twill not go against the hair: you see I can make no more music than a beetle of a cow-turd.

Cud. Let me see, Father Sawgut [*Takes the fiddle*]; say once you had a brave hobby-horse that you were beholding to. I'll play and dance too. —Ningle, away with it. [*Gives it to the Dog, who plays the morris.*

All the Clowns. Ay, marry, sir! [*They dance.*

Enter a Constable and Officers.

Con. Away with jollity! 'tis too sad an hour.—
Sir Arthur Clarington, your own assistance,
In the king's name, I charge, for apprehension
Of these two murderers, Warbeck and Somerton.

Sir Arth. Ha! flat murderers?

Som. Ha, ha, ha! this has awakened my melancholy.

War. And struck my mirth down flat.—Murderers?

Con. The accusation's flat against you, gentlemen.—
Sir, you may be satisfied with this. [*Shows his warrant.*]—
I hope you'll quietly obey my power;
'Twill make your cause the fairer.

Som. and War. O, with all our hearts, sir.

Cud. There's my rival taken up for hangman's meat; Tom told me he was about a piece of villany.—Mates and morris-men, you see here's no longer piping, no longer dancing; this news of murder has slain the morris. You that go the footway, fare ye well; I am for a gallop.—Come, ningle. [*Canters off with the Hobby-horse and the Dog.*

Saw. [*Strikes his fiddle, which sounds as before.*] Ay? nay, an my fiddle be come to himself again, I care not. I think the devil has been abroad amongst us to-day; I'll keep thee out of thy fit now, if I can.

[*Exit with the Morris-dancers.*

Sir Arth. These things are full of horror, full of pity.
But if this time be constant to the proof,
The guilt of both these gentlemen I dare take
On mine own danger; yet, howsoever, sir,
Your power must be obeyed.

War. O, most willingly, sir.
'Tis a most sweet affliction; I could not meet
A joy in the best shape with better will:
Come, fear not, sir; nor judge nor evidence
Can bind him o'er who's freed by conscience.

Som. Mine stands so upright to the middle zone
It takes no shadow to't, it goes alone. [*Exeunt.*

ACT THE FOURTH.

SCENE I.—*Edmonton. The Street.*

Enter Old Banks *and several Countrymen.*

Old Banks. My horse this morning runs most piteously of the glanders, whose nose yesternight was as clean as any man's here now coming from the barber's; and this, I'll take my death upon't, is long of this jadish witch Mother Sawyer.

1st Coun. I took my wife and a serving-man in our town of Edmonton thrashing in my barn together such corn as country wenches carry to market; and examining my polecat why she did so, she swore in her conscience she was bewitched: and what witch have we about us but Mother Sawyer?

2nd Coun. Rid the town of her, else all our wives will do nothing else but dance about other country maypoles.

3rd Coun. Our cattle fall, our wives fall, our daughters fall, and maid-servants fall; and we ourselves shall not be able to stand, if this beast be suffered to graze amongst us.

Enter Hamluc *with thatch and a lighted link.*

Ham. Burn the witch, the witch, the witch, the witch!

Countrymen. What hast got there?

Ham. A handful of thatch plucked off a hovel of hers; and they say, when 'tis burning, if she be a witch, she'll come running in.

O. Banks. Fire it, fire it! I'll stand between thee and home for any danger. [Ham. *sets fire to the thatch.*

Enter Mother Sawyer *running.*

M. Saw. Diseases, plagues, the curse of an old woman
Follow and fall upon you!

Countrymen. Are you come, you old trot?

O. Banks. You hot whore, must we fetch you with fire in your tail?

1st Coun. This thatch is as good as a jury to prove she is a witch.

Countrymen. Out, witch! beat her, kick her, set fire on her!

M. Saw. Shall I be murdered by a bed of serpents? Help, help!

Enter SIR ARTHUR CLARINGTON *and a Justice.*

Countrymen. Hang her, beat her, kill her!

Just. How now! forbear this violence.

M. Saw. A crew of villains, a knot of bloody hangmen,
Set to torment me, I know not why.

Just. Alas, neighbour Banks, are you a ringleader in mischief? fie! to abuse an aged woman.

O. Banks. Woman? a she hell-cat, a witch! To prove her one, we no sooner set fire on the thatch of her house, but in she came running as if the devil had sent her in a barrel of gunpowder; which trick as surely proves her a witch as the pox in a snuffling nose is a sign a man is a whore-master.

Just. Come, come: firing her thatch? ridiculous!
Take heed, sirs, what you do; unless your proofs
Come better armed, instead of turning her
Into a witch, you'll prove yourselves stark fools.

Countrymen. Fools?

Just. Arrant fools.

O. Banks. Pray, Master Justice What-do-you-call-'em, hear me but in one thing: this grumbling devil owes me I know no good-will ever since I fell out with her.

M. Saw. And break'dst my back with beating me.

O. Banks. I'll break it worse.

M. Saw. Wilt thou?

Just. You must not threaten her; 'tis against law: Go on.

O. Banks. So, sir, ever since, having a dun cow tied up in my backside,[36] let me go thither, or but cast mine eye at her, and if I should be hanged I cannot choose, though it be ten times in an hour, but run to the cow, and taking up her tail, kiss—saving your worship's reverence—my cow behind, that the whole town of Edmonton has been ready to bepiss themselves with laughing me to scorn.

Just. And this is long of her?

O. Banks. Who the devil else? for is any man such an ass to be such a baby, if he were not bewitched?

Sir Arth. Nay, if she be a witch, and the harms she does end in such sports, she may scape burning.

Just. Go, go: pray, vex her not; she is a subject,
And you must not be judges of the law
To strike her as you please.

Countrymen. No, no, we'll find cudgel enough to strike her.

O. Banks. Ay; no lips to kiss but my cow's—!

M. Saw. Rots and foul maladies eat up thee and thine! [*Exeunt* OLD BANKS *and Countrymen.*

Just. Here's none now, Mother Sawyer, but this gentleman,
Myself, and you: let us to some mild questions;
Have you mild answers; tell us honestly
And with a free confession—we'll do our best
To wean you from it—are you a witch, or no?

M. Saw. I am none.

Just. Be not so furious.

M. Saw. I am none.
None but base curs so bark at me; I'm none:
Or would I were! if every poor old woman
Be trod on thus by slaves, reviled, kicked, beaten,
As I am daily, she to be revenged
Had need turn witch.

Sir Arth. And you to be revenged
Have sold your soul to th' devil.

[36]An outbuilding or yard in the rear of a house.

M. Saw. Keep thine own from him.

Just. You are too saucy and too bitter.

M. Saw. Saucy?
By what commission can he send my soul
On the devil's errand more than I can his?
Is he a landlord of my soul, to thrust it,
When he list, out of door?

Just. Know whom you speak to.

M. Saw. A man; perhaps no man. Men in gay clothes,
Whose backs are laden with titles and with honours,
Are within far more crookèd than I am,
And, if I be a witch, more witch-like.

Sir Arth. You're a base hell-hound.—
And now, sir, let me tell you, far and near
She's bruited for a woman that maintains
A spirit that sucks her.

M. Saw. I defy thee.

Sir Arth. Go, go:
I can, if need be, bring an hundred voices,
E'en here in Edmonton, that shall loud proclaim
Thee for a secret and pernicious witch.

M. Saw. Ha, ha!

Just. Do you laugh? why laugh you?

M. Saw. At my name,
The brave name this knight gives me—witch.

Just. Is the name of witch so pleasing to thine ear?

Sir Arth. Pray, sir, give way, and let her tongue gallop on.

M. Saw. A witch! who is not?
Hold not that universal name in scorn, then.
What are your painted things in princes' courts,
Upon whose eyelids lust sits, blowing fires
To burn men's souls in sensual hot desires,
Upon whose naked paps a lecher's thought

Acts sin in fouler shapes than can be wrought?

Just. But those work not as you do.

M. Saw. No, but far worse
These by enchantments can whole lordships change
To trunks of rich attire, turn ploughs and teams
To Flanders mares and coaches, and huge trains
Of servitors to a French butterfly.
Have you not city-witches who can turn
Their husbands' wares, whole standing shops of wares,
To sumptuous tables, gardens of stolen sin;
In one year wasting what scarce twenty win?
Are not these witches?

Just. Yes, yes; but the law
Casts not an eye on these.

M. Saw. Why, then, on me,
Or any lean old beldam? Reverence once
Had wont to wait on age; now an old woman,
Ill-favoured grown with years, if she be poor,
Must be called bawd or witch. Such so abused
Are the coarse witches; t'other are the fine,
Spun for the devil's own wearing.

Sir Arth. And so is thine.

M. Saw. She on whose tongue a whirlwind sits to blow
A man out of himself, from his soft pillow
To lean his head on rocks and fighting waves,
Is not that scold a witch? The man of law
Whose honeyed hopes the credulous client draw—
As bees by tinkling basins—to swarm to him
From his own hive to work the wax in his;
He is no witch, not he!

Sir Arth. But these men-witches
Are not in trading with hell's merchandise,
Like such as you are, that for a word, a look,
Denial of a coal of fire, kill men,
Children, and cattle.

M. Saw. Tell them, sir, that do so:
Am I accused for such an one?

Sir Arth. Yes; 'twill be sworn.

M. Saw. Dare any swear I ever tempted maiden
With golden hooks flung at her chastity
To come and lose her honour; and being lost,
To pay not a denier[37] for't? Some slaves have done it.
Men-witches can, without the fangs of law
Drawing once one drop of blood, put counterfeit pieces
Away for true gold.

Sir Arth. By one thing she speaks
I know now she's a witch, and dare no longer
Hold conference with the fury.

Just. Let's, then, away.—
Old woman, mend thy life; get home and pray. [*Exeunt* SIR ARTHUR *and Justice.*

M. Saw. For his confusion.

Enter the Dog.

My dear Tom-boy, welcome!
I'm torn in pieces by a pack of curs
Clapt all upon me, and for want of thee:
Comfort me; thou shall have the teat anon.

Dog. Bow, wow! I'll have it now.

M. Saw. I am dried up
With cursing and with madness, and have yet
No blood to moisten these sweet lips of thine.
Stand on thy hind-legs up—kiss me, my Tommy,
And rub away some wrinkles on my brow
By making my old ribs to shrug for joy
Of thy fine tricks. What hast thou done? let's tickle.
Hast thou struck the horse lame as I bid thee?

Dog. Yes;
And nipped the sucking child.

M. Saw. Ho, ho, my dainty,
My little pearl! no lady loves her hound,
Monkey, or paroquet, as I do thee.

---

[37]Penny. Lat. *Denarius.*

Dog. The maid has been churning butter nine hours; but it shall not come.

M. Saw. Let 'em eat cheese and choke.

Dog. I had rare sport
Among the clowns i' th' morris.

M. Saw. I could dance
Out of my skin to hear thee. But, my curl-pate,
That jade, that foul-tongued whore, Nan Ratcliffe,
Who, for a little soap licked by my sow,
Struck and almost had lamed it;—did not I charge thee
To pinch that queen to th' heart?

Dog. Bow, wow, wow! look here else.

Enter ANN RATCLIFFE *mad.*

Ann. See, see, see! the man i' th' moon has built a new windmill; and what running there's from all quarters of the city to learn the art of grinding!

M. Saw. Ho, ho, ho! I thank thee, my sweet mongrel.

Ann. Hoyda! a pox of the devil's false hopper! all the golden meal runs into the rich knaves' purses, and the poor have nothing but bran. Hey derry down! are not you Mother Sawyer?

M. Saw. No, I am a lawyer.

Ann. Art thou? I prithee let me scratch thy face; for thy pen has flayed-off a great many men's skins. You'll have brave doings in the vacation; for knaves and fools are at variance in every village. I'll sue Mother Sawyer, and her own sow shall give in evidence against her.

M. Saw. Touch her. [*To the Dog, who rubs against her.*

Ann. O, my ribs are made of a paned hose, and they break![38] There's a Lancashire hornpipe in my throat; hark, how it tickles it, with doodle, doodle, doodle, doodle! Welcome, sergeants! welcome, devil!—hands, hands! hold hands, and dance around, around, around. [*Dancing.*

Re-enter OLD BANKS, *with* CUDDY, RATCLIFFE, *and Countrymen.*

---

[38]Paned hose were made of stripes (panels) of different-coloured stuff stitched together, and therefore liable to break or be seam-rent. Thus counterpane.

Rat. She's here; alas, my poor wife is here!

O. Banks. Catch her fast, and have her into some close chamber, do; for she's, as many wives are, stark mad.

Cud. The witch! Mother Sawyer, the witch, the devil!

Rat. O, my dear wife! help, sirs! [ANN *is carried off by* RATCLIFFE *and Countrymen.*

O. Banks. You see your work, Mother Bumby.[39]

M. Saw. My work? should she and all you here run mad,
Is the work mine?

Cud. No, on my conscience, she would not hurt a devil of two years old.

Re-enter RATCLIFFE *and Countrymen.*

How now! what's become of her?

Rat. Nothing; she's become nothing but the miserable trunk of a wretched woman. We were in her hands as reeds in a mighty tempest: spite of our strengths away she brake; and nothing in her mouth being heard but "the devil, the witch, the witch, the devil!" she beat out her own brains, and so died.

Cud. It's any man's case, be he never so wise, to die when his brains go a wool-gathering.

O. Banks. Masters, be ruled by me; let's all to a justice.—Hag, thou hast done this, and thou shalt answer it.

M. Saw. Banks, I defy thee.

O. Banks. Get a warrant first to examine her, then ship her to Newgate; here's enough, if all her other villanies were pardoned, to burn her for a witch.—You have a spirit, they say, comes to you in the likeness of a dog; we shall see your cur at one time or other: if we do, unless it be the devil himself, he shall go howling to the gaol in one chain, and thou in another.

---

[39]Farmer Banks is very familiar with the names of old plays (or rather of the supposed witches who gave names to the plays). *Mother Bombie* is the title of one of Lyly's comedies, of which she is the heroine; as is *Gammer Gurton* of the farcical drama, *Gammer Gurton's Needle*, to which Old Banks presently refers.

M. Saw. Be hanged thou in a third, and do thy worst!

Cud. How, father! you send the poor dumb thing howling to the gaol? he that makes him howl makes me roar.

O. Banks. Why, foolish boy, dost thou know him?

Cud. No matter if I do or not: he's bailable, I am sure, by law;—but if the dog's word will not be taken, mine shall.

O. Banks. Thou bail for a dog!

Cud. Yes, or a bitch either, being my friend. I'll lie by the heels myself before puppison shall; his dog days are not come yet, I hope.

O. Banks. What manner of dog is it? didst ever see him?

Cud. See him? yes, and given him a bone to gnaw twenty times. The dog is no court-foisting hound that fills his belly full by base wagging his tail; neither is it a citizen's water-spaniel,[40] enticing his master to go a-ducking twice or thrice a week, whilst his wife makes ducks and drakes at home: this is no Paris-garden bandog[41] neither, that keeps a bow-wow-wowing to have butchers bring their curs thither; and when all comes to all, they run away like sheep: neither is this the Black Dog of Newgate.[42]

O. Banks. No, Goodman Son-fool, but the dog of hell-gate.

Cud. I say, Goodman Father-fool, it's a lie.

All. He's bewitched.

Cud. A gross lie, as big as myself. The devil in St. Dunstan's will as soon drink with this poor cur as with any Temple-bar laundress that washes and wrings lawyers.

Dog. Bow, wow, wow, wow!

---

[40]A breed of dogs, in great request for hunting ducks in the ponds at Islington and other outlying regions of London at this period.

[41]A fierce kind of mastiff kept to bait bears. Paris garden, where these brutal sports were regularly exhibited, was situated on the Bankside in Southwark, close to the Globe Theatre.—*Gifford.*

[42]There is a tract, in prose and verse, attributed to Luke Hatton, entitled *The Black Dog of Newgate*; and we learn from Henslowe's *Diary* that there was a play by Hathway, Day, Smith, and another poet, with the same title.—*Dyce.*

All. O, the dog's here, the dog's here.

O. Banks. It was the voice of a dog.

Cud. The voice of a dog? if that voice were a dog's, what voice had my mother? so am I a dog: bow, wow, wow! It was I that barked so, father, to make coxcombs of these clowns.

O. Banks. However, we'll be coxcombed no longer: away, therefore, to the justice for a warrant; and then, Gammer Gurton, have at your needle of witchcraft!

M. Saw. And prick thine own eyes out. Go, peevish fools! [*Exeunt* OLD BANKS, RATCLIFFE, *and Countrymen.*

Cud. Ningle, you had liked to have spoiled all with your bow-ings. I was glad to have put 'em off with one of my dog-tricks on a sudden; I am bewitched, little Cost me-nought, to love thee—a pox,—that morris makes me spit in thy mouth.—I dare not stay; farewell, ningle; you whoreson dog's nose!—Farewell, witch! [*Exit.*

Dog. Bow, wow, wow, wow.

M. Saw. Mind him not, he is not worth thy worrying;
Run at a fairer game: that foul-mouthed knight,
Scurvy Sir Arthur, fly at him, my Tommy,
And pluck out's throat.

Dog. No, there's a dog already biting,—'s conscience.

M. Saw. That's a sure bloodhound. Come, let's home and play;
Our black work ended, we'll make holiday. [*Exeunt.*

SCENE II. *A Bedroom in* CARTER'S *House. A bed thrust forth, with* FRANK *in a slumber.*

Enter KATHERINE.

Kath. Brother, brother! so sound asleep? that's well.

Frank. [*Waking.*] No, not I, sister; he that's wounded here
As I am—all my other hurts are bitings
Of a poor flea;—but he that here once bleeds
Is maimed incurably.

Kath. My good sweet brother,—
For now my sister must grow up in you,—
Though her loss strikes you through, and that I feel
The blow as deep, I pray thee be not cruel
To kill me too, by seeing you cast away
In your own helpless sorrow. Good love, sit up;
And if you can give physic to yourself,
I shall be well.

Frank. I'll do my best.

Kath. I thank you;
What do you look about for?

Frank. Nothing, nothing;
But I was thinking, sister,—

Kath. Dear heart, what?

Frank. Who but a fool would thus be bound to a bed,
Having this room to walk in?

Kath. Why do you talk so?
Would you were fast asleep!

Frank. No, no; I'm not idle.[43]
But here's my meaning; being robbed as I am,
Why should my soul, which married was to hers,
Live in divorce, and not fly after her?
Why should I not walk hand in hand with Death,
To find my love out?

Kath. That were well indeed,
Your time being come; when Death is sent to call you,
No doubt you shall meet her.

Frank. Why should not I
Go without calling?

Kath. Yes, brother, so you might,
Were there no place to go when you're gone
But only this.

Frank. 'Troth, sister, thou say'st true;
For when a man has been an hundred years

[43] *i.e.* Wandering.

Hard travelling o'er the tottering bridge of age,
He's not the thousand part upon his way:
All life is but a wandering to find home;
When we're gone, we're there. Happy were man,
Could here his voyage end; he should not, then,
Answer how well or ill he steered his soul
By Heaven's or by Hell's compass; how he put in—
Losing blessed goodness' shore—at such a sin;
Nor how life's dear provision he has spent,
Nor how far he in's navigation went
Beyond commission: this were a fine reign,
To do ill and not hear of it again;
Yet then were man more wretched than a beast;
For, sister, our dead pay is sure the best.

Kath. 'Tis so, the best or worst; and I wish Heaven
To pay—and so I know it will—that traitor,
That devil Somerton—who stood in mine eye
Once as an angel—home to his deservings:
What villain but himself, once loving me,
With Warbeck's soul would pawn his own to hell
To be revenged on my poor sister!

Frank. Slaves!
A pair of merciless slaves! speak no more of them.

Kath. I think this talking hurts you.

Frank. Does me no good, I'm sure;
I pay for't everywhere.

Kath. I have done, then.
Eat, if you cannot sleep; you have these two days
Not tasted any food.—Jane, is it ready?

Frank. What's ready? what's ready?

Kath. I have made ready a roasted chicken for you:

Enter Maid with chicken.

Sweet, wilt thou eat?

Frank. A pretty stomach on a sudden; yes.—
There's one in the house can play upon a lute;
Good girl, let's hear him too.

Kath. You shall, dear brother. [*Exit Maid.*

Would I were a musician, you should hear
How I would feast your ear! [*Lute plays within*]—stay mend your pillow,
And raise you higher.

Frank. I am up too high,
Am I not, sister now?

Kath. No, no; 'tis well.
Fall-to, fall-to.—A knife! here's never a knife.
Brother, I'll look out yours. [*Takes up his vest.*

Enter the Dog, *shrugging as it were for joy, and dances.*

Frank. Sister, O, sister,
I'm ill upon a sudden, and can eat nothing.

Kath. In very deed you shall: the want of food
Makes you so faint, Ha! [*Sees the bloody knife*]—here's none in your pocket;
I'll go fetch a knife. [*Exit hastily.*

Frank. Will you?—'tis well, all's well.

FRANK *searches first one pocket, then the other, finds the knife, and then lies down.—The Dog runs off.—The spirit of* SUSAN *comes to the bed's side;* FRANK *stares at it, and then turns to the other side, but the spirit is there too. Meanwhile enter* WINNIFRED *as a page, and stands sadly at the bed's foot.—*FRANK *affrighted sits up. The spirit vanishes.*

Frank. What art thou?

Win. A lost creature.

Frank. So am I too.—Win?
Ah, my she-page!

Win. For your sake I put on
A shape that's false; yet do I wear a heart
True to you as your own.

Frank. Would mine and thine
Were fellows in one house!—Kneel by me here.
On this side now! how dar'st thou come to mock me

On both sides of my bed?

Win. When?

Frank. But just now:
Outface me, stare upon me with strange postures,
Turn my soul wild by a face in which were drawn
A thousand ghosts leapt newly from their graves
To pluck me into a winding-sheet!

Win. Believe it,
I came no nearer to you than yon place
At your bed's feet; and of the house had leave,
Calling myself your horse-boy, in to come,
And visit my sick master.

Frank. Then 'twas my fancy;
Some windmill in my brains for want of sleep.

Win. Would I might never sleep, so you could rest!
But you have plucked a thunder on your head,
Whose noise cannot cease suddenly: why should you
Dance at the wedding of a second wife,
When scarce the music which you heard at mine
Had ta'en a farewell of you? O, this was ill!
And they who thus can give both hands away
In th' end shall want their best limbs.

Frank. Winnifred,—
The chamber-door's fast?

Win. Yes.

Frank. Sit thee, then, down;
And when thou'st heard me speak, melt into tears:
Yet I, to save those eyes of thine from weeping,
Being to write a story of us two.
Instead of ink dipped my sad pen in blood.
When of thee I took leave, I went abroad
Only for pillage, as a freebooter,
What gold soe'er I got to make it thine.
To please a father I have Heaven displeased;
Striving to cast two wedding-rings in one,
Through my bad workmanship I now have none;
I have lost her and thee.

Win. I know she's dead;
But you have me still.

Frank. Nay, her this hand
Murdered; and so I lose thee too.

Win. O me!

Frank. Be quiet; for thou my evidence art,
Jury, and judge: sit quiet, and I'll tell all.

While they are conversing in a low tone, enter at one door CARTER and KATHERINE, *at the other the Dog, pawing softly at* FRANK.

Kath. I have run madding up and down to find you,
Being laden with the heaviest news that ever
Poor daughter carried.

Car. Why? is the boy dead?

Kath. Dead, sir!
O, father, we are cozened: you are told
The murderer sings in prison, and he laughs here.
This villain killed my sister see else, see,

[*Takes up his vest, and shows the knife to her father, who secures it.*

A bloody knife in's pocket!

Car. Bless me, patience!

Frank. [*Seeing them.*] The knife, the knife, the knife!

Kath. What knife? [*Exit the Dog.*

Frank. To cut my chicken up, my chicken;
Be you my carver, father.

Car. That I will.

Kath. How the devil steels our brows after doing ill!

Frank. My stomach and my sight are taken from me;
All is not well within me.

Car. I believe thee, boy; I that have seen so many moons clap their horns on other men's foreheads to strike them sick, yet mine to scape and be well; I that never cast away a fee upon urinals, but am as sound as an honest man's conscience when he's dying; I should cry out as thou dost, "All is not well within me," felt I but the bag of thy imposthumes. Ah, poor villain! ah, my wounded rascal! all my grief is, I have now small hope of thee.

Frank. Do the surgeons say my wounds are dangerous, then?

Car. Yes, yes, and there's no way with thee but one.

Frank. Would he were here to open them!

Car. I'll go to fetch him; I'll make an holiday to see thee as I wish.

Frank. A wondrous kind old man!

Win. [*Aside to* FRANK.] Your sin's the blacker
So to abuse his goodness.—[*Aloud*] Master, how do you?

Frank. Pretty well now, boy; I have such odd qualms
Come cross my stomach.—I'll fall-to; boy, cut me—

Win. [*Aside.*] You have cut me, I'm sure;—A leg or wing, sir?

Frank. No, no, no; a wing—
[*Aside.*] Would I had wings but to soar up yon tower!
But here's a clog that hinders me.

Re-enter CARTER, *with Servants bearing the body of* SUSAN *in a coffin.*

What's that?

Car. That! what? O, now I see her; 'tis a young wench, my daughter, sirrah, sick to the death; and hearing thee to be an excellent rascal for letting blood, she looks out at a casement, and cries, "Help, help! stay that man! him I must have or none."

Frank. For pity's sake, remove her: see, she stares
With one broad open eye still in my face!

Car. Thou putted'st both hers out, like a villain as thou art; yet, see! she is willing to lend thee one again to find out the murderer, and that's thyself.

Frank. Old man, thou liest!

Car. So shalt thou—in the gaol.—
Run for officers.

Kath. O, thou merciless slave!
She was—though yet above ground—in her grave
To me; but thou hast torn it up again—
Mine eyes, too much drowned, now must feel more rain.

Car. Fetch officers.

[*Exit* KATHERINE *and Servants with the body of* SUSAN.

Frank. For whom?

Car. For thee, sirrah, sirrah! Some knives have foolish posies upon them, but thine has a villainous one; look! [*Showing the bloody knife.*] O, it is enamelled with the heart-blood of thy hated wife, my belovèd daughter! What sayest thou to this evidence? is't not sharp? does't not strike home? Thou canst not answer honestly and without a trembling heart to this one point, this terrible bloody point.

Win. I beseech you, sir,
Strike him no more; you see he's dead already.

Car. O, sir, you held his horses; you are as arrant a rogue as he: up go you too.

Frank. As you're a man, throw not upon that woman
Your loads of tyranny, for she is innocent.

Car. How! how! a woman! Is't grown to a fashion for women in all countries to wear the breeches?

Win. I'm not as my disguise speaks me, sir, his page,
But his first, only wife, his lawful wife.

Car. How! how! more fire i' th' bed-straw![44]

Win. The wrongs which singly fell upon your daughter
On me are multiplied; she lost a life,
But I an husband, and myself must lose
If you call him to a bar for what he has done.

Car. He has done it, then?

Win. Yes, 'tis confessed to me.

Frank. Dost thou betray me?

[44]A proverbial expression for more concealed mischief.—*Gifford.*

Win. O, pardon me, dear heart! I'm mad to lose thee,
And know not what I speak; but if thou didst,
I must arraign this father for two sins,
Adultery and murder.

Re-enter KATHERINE.

Kath. Sir, they are come.

Car. Arraign me for what thou wilt, all Middlesex knows me better for an honest man than the middle of a market-place knows thee for an honest woman.—Rise, sirrah, and don your tacklings; rig yourself for the gallows, or I'll carry thee thither on my back: your trull shall to the gaol go with you: there be as fine Newgate birds as she that can draw him in: pox on's wounds!

Frank. I have served thee, and my wages now are paid;
Yet my worse punishment shall, I hope, be stayed. [*Exeunt.*

ACT THE FIFTH.

SCENE I.—*The Witch's Cottage.*

Enter MOTHER SAWYER.

MOTHER SAWYER. Still wronged by every slave, and not a dog
Bark in his dame's defence? I am called witch,
Yet am myself bewitched from doing harm.
Have I given up myself to thy black lust
Thus to be scorned? Not see me in three days!
I'm lost without my Tomalin; prithee come,
Revenge to me is sweeter far than life;
Thou art my raven, on whose coal-black wings
Revenge comes flying to me. O, my best love!
I am on fire, even in the midst of ice,
Raking my blood up, till my shrunk knees feel
Thy curled head leaning on them: come, then, my darling;
If in the air thou hover'st, fall upon me
In some dark cloud; and as I oft have seen
Dragons and serpents in the elements,
Appear thou now so to me. Art thou i' th' sea?
Muster-up all the monsters from the deep,
And be the ugliest of them: so that my bulch[45]
Show but his swarth cheek to me, let earth cleave
And break from hell, I care not! Could I run
Like a swift powder-mine beneath the world,
Up would I blow it all, to find out thee,
Though I lay ruined in it. Not yet come!
I must, then, fall to my old prayer:
Sanctibicetur nomen tuum.

Not yet come! the worrying of wolves, biting of mad dogs, the manges, and the—

Enter the Dog *which is now white.*

Dog. How now! whom art thou cursing?

M. Saw. Thee!

---

[45]Literally, a bull-calf, sometimes used, as here, as an expression of kindness; but generally indicative of familiarity and contempt.—*Gifford.*

Ha! no, it is my black cur I am cursing
For not attending on me.

Dog. I am that cur.

M. Saw. Thou liest: hence! come not nigh me.

Dog. Baw, waw!

M. Saw. Why dost thou thus appear to me in white,
As if thou wert the ghost of my dear love?

Dog. I am dogged, and list not to tell thee; yet,—to torment thee,—my whiteness puts thee in mind of thy winding-sheet.

M. Saw. Am I near death?

Dog. Yes, if the dog of hell be near thee; when the devil comes to thee as a lamb, have at thy throat!

M. Saw. Off, cur!

Dog. He has the back of a sheep, but the belly of an otter; devours by sea and land. "Why am I in white?" didst thou not pray to me?

M. Saw. Yes, thou dissembling hell-hound!
Why now in white more than at other times?

Dog. Be blasted with the news! whiteness is day's footboy, a forerunner to light, which shows thy old rivelled face: villanies are stripped naked; the witch must be beaten out of her cockpit.

M. Saw. Must she? she shall not: thou'rt a lying spirit:
Why to mine eyes art thou a flag of truce?
I am at peace with none; 'tis the black colour,
Or none, which I fight under: I do not like
Thy puritan paleness; glowing furnaces
Are far more hot than they which flame outright.
If thou my old dog art, go and bite such
As I shall set thee on.

Dog. I will not.

M. Saw. I'll sell myself to twenty thousand fiends
To have thee torn in pieces, then.

Dog. Thou canst not; thou art so ripe to fall into hell, that no more of my kennel will so much as bark at him that hangs thee.

M. Saw. I shall run mad.

Dog. Do so, thy time is come to curse, and rave, and die; the glass of thy sins is full, and it must run out at gallows.

M. Saw. It cannot, ugly cur; I'll confess nothing;
And not confessing, who dare come and swear
I have bewitched them? I'll not confess one mouthful.

Dog. Choose, and be hanged or burned.

M. Saw. Spite of the devil and thee,
I'll muzzle up my tongue from telling tales.

Dog. Spite of thee and the devil, thou'lt be condemned.

M. Saw. Yes! when?

Dog. And ere the executioner catch thee full in's claws, thou'lt confess all.

M. Saw. Out, dog!

Dog. Out, witch! thy trial is at hand:
Our prey being had, the devil does laughing stand. [*Runs aside.*

Enter OLD BANKS, RATCLIFFE, *and Countrymen.*

O. Banks. She's here: attach her.— Witch you must go with us. [*They seize her.*

M. Saw. Whither? to hell?

O. Banks. No, no, no, old crone; your mittimus shall be made thither, but your own jailors shall receive you.—Away with her!

M. Saw. My Tommy! my sweet Tom-boy! O, thou dog!
Dost thou now fly to thy kennel and forsake me?
Plagues and consumptions—[*She is carried off.*

Dog. Ha, ha, ha, ha!
Let not the world witches or devils condemn;
They follow us, and then we follow them.

Enter CUDDY BANKS.

Cud. I would fain meet with mine ningle once more: he has had a claw amongst 'em: my rival that loved my wench is like to be hanged like an innocent. A kind cur where he takes, but where he takes not, a dogged rascal; I know the villain loves me. [*The Dog barks.*] No! art thou there? [*Seeing the Dog.*] that's Tom's voice, but 'tis not he; this is a dog of another hair, this. Bark, and not speak to me? not Tom, then; there's as much difference betwixt Tom and this as betwixt white and black.

Dog. Hast thou forgot me?

Cud. That's Tom again.—Prithee, ningle, speak; is thy name Tom?

Dog. Whilst I served my old Dame Sawyer 'twas; I'm gone from her now.

Cud. Gone? Away with the witch, then, too! she'll never thrive if thou leavest her; she knows no more how to kill a cow, or a horse, or a sow, without thee, than she does to kill a goose.

Dog. No, she has done killing now, but must be killed for what she has done; she's shortly to be hanged.

Cud. Is she? in my conscience, if she be, 'tis thou hast brought her to the gallows, Tom.

Dog. Right; I served her to that purpose; 'twas part of my wages.

Cud. This was no honest servant's part, by your leave, Tom. This remember, I pray you, between you and I; I entertained you ever as a dog, not as a devil.

Dog. True;
And so I used thee doggedly, not devilishly;
I have deluded thee for sport to laugh at:
The wench thou seek'st after thou never spak'st with,
But a spirit in her form, habit, and likeness.
Ha, ha!

Cud. I do not, then, wonder at the change of your garments, if you can enter into shapes of women too.

Dog. Any shape, to blind such silly eyes as thine; but chiefly those coarse creatures, dog, or cat, hare, ferret, frog, toad.

Cud. Louse or flea?

Dog. Any poor vermin.

Cud. It seems you devils have poor thin souls, that you can bestow yourselves in such small bodies. But, pray you, Tom, one question at parting;—I think I shall never see you more;—where do you borrow those bodies that are none of your own?—the garment-shape you may hire at broker's.

Dog. Why would'st thou know that, fool? it avails thee not.

Cud. Only for my mind's sake, Tom, and to tell some of my friends.

Dog. I'll thus much tell thee: thou never art so distant
From an evil spirit, but that thy oaths,
Curses, and blasphemies pull him to thine elbow;
Thou never tell'st a lie, but that a devil
Is within hearing it; thy evil purposes
Are ever haunted; but when they come to act,—
As thy tongue slandering, bearing false witness,
Thy hand stabbing, stealing, cozening, cheating,—
He's then within thee: thou play'st, he bets upon thy part;
Although thou lose, yet he will gain by thee.

Cud. Ay? then he comes in the shape of a rook?

Dog. The old cadaver of some self-strangled wretch
We sometimes borrow, and appear human;
The carcass of some disease-slain strumpet
We varnish fresh, and wear as her first beauty.
Did'st never hear? if not, it has been done;
An hot luxurious lecher in his twines,
When he has thought to clip his dalliance,
There has provided been for his embrace
A fine hot flaming devil in her place.

Cud. Yes, I am partly a witness to this; but I never could embrace her; I thank thee for that, Tom. Well, again I thank thee, Tom, for all this counsel; without a fee too! there's few lawyers of thy mind now. Certainly, Tom, I begin to pity thee.

Dog. Pity me! for what?

Cud. Were it not possible for thee to become an honest dog yet?—'Tis a base life that you lead, Tom, to serve witches, to kill innocent children, to kill harmless cattle, to stroy[46] corn and fruit, etc.: 'twere better yet to be a butcher and kill for yourself.

Dog. Why, these are all my delights, my pleasures, fool.

Cud. Or, Tom, if you could give your mind to ducking,—I know you can swim, fetch, and carry,—some shop-keeper in London would take great delight in you, and be a tender master over you: or if you have a mind to the game either at bull or bear, I think I could prefer you to Moll Cutpurse[47].

Dog. Ha, ha! I should kill all the game,—bulls, bears, dogs and all; not a cub to be left.

Cud. You could do, Tom; but you must play fair; you should be staved-off else. Or if your stomach did better like to serve in some nobleman's, knight's, or gentleman's kitchen, if you could brook the wheel and turn the spit—your labour could not be much—when they have roast meat, that's but once or twice in the week at most: here you might lick your own toes very well. Or if you could translate yourself into a lady's arming puppy, there you might lick sweet lips, and do many pretty offices; but to creep under an old witch's coats, and suck like a great puppy! fie upon't!—I have heard beastly things of you, Tom.

Dog. Ha, ha!
The worse thou heard'st of me the better 'tis.
Shall I serve thee, fool, at the selfsame rate?

Cud. No, I'll see thee hanged, thou shalt be damned first! I know thy qualities too well, I'll give no suck to such whelps; therefore henceforth I defy thee. Out, and avaunt!

Dog. Nor will I serve for such a silly soul:
I am for greatness now, corrupted greatness;
There I'll shug in,[48] and get a noble countenance;[49]

---

[46]*i.e.* Destroy.

[47]A notorious character of those days, whose real name was Mary Frith. She appears to have excelled in various professions, of which far the most honest and praiseworthy was that of picking pockets. By singular good fortune she escaped the gallows, and died, "in a ripe and rotten old age," some time before the Restoration. Moll is the heroine of *The Roaring Girl*, a lively comedy by Middleton and Dekker, who have treated her with kindness.—*Gifford.*

[48]Creep in.

[49]Patronage, protection, responsibility.—*Gifford.*

Serve some Briarean footcloth-strider,[50]
That has an hundred hands to catch at bribes,
But not a finger's nail of charity.
Such, like the dragon's tail, shall pull down hundreds
To drop and sink with him:[51] I'll stretch myself,
And draw this bulk small as a silver wire,
Enter at the least pore tobacco-fume
Can make a breach for:—hence, silly fool!
I scorn to prey on such an atom soul.

Cud. Come out, come out, you cur! I will beat thee out of the bounds of Edmonton, and to-morrow we go in procession, and after thou shalt never come in again: if thou goest to London, I'll make thee go about by Tyburn, stealing in by Thieving Lane. If thou canst rub thy shoulder against a lawyer's gown, as thou passest by Westminster-hall, do; if not, to the stairs amongst the bandogs, take water, and the Devil go with thee! [*Exit, followed by the Dog barking.*

SCENE II.—*London. The neighbourhood of Tyburn.*

Enter Justice, Sir Arthur, Somerton, Warbeck, Carter, *and* Katherine.

Just. Sir Arthur, though the bench hath mildly censured your errors, yet you have indeed been the instrument that wrought all their misfortunes; I would wish you paid down your fine speedily and willingly.

Sir Arth. I'll need no urging to it.

Car. If you should, 'twere a shame to you; for if I should speak my conscience, you are worthier to be hanged of the two, all things considered; and now make what you can of it: but I am glad these gentlemen are freed.

War. We knew our innocence.

Som. And therefore feared it not.

[50]Footcloths were the ornamental housings or trappings flung over the pads of state-horses. On these the great lawyers then rode to Westminster Hall, and, as our authors intimate, the great courtiers to St. James's. They became common enough in aftertimes.—*Gifford.* Briareus, the hundred-handed giant. The allusion is obvious.

[51]Compare "Revelation." ch. xii.

Kath. But I am glad that I have you safe. [*A noise within.*

Just. How now! what noise is that?

Car. Young Frank is going the wrong way. Alas, poor youth! now I begin to pity him.

Enter Old Thorney *and* Winnifred *weeping.*

O. Thor. Here let our sorrows wait him; to press nearer
The place of his sad death, some apprehensions
May tempt our grief too much, at height already.—
Daughter be comforted.

Win. Comfort and I
Are far too separated to be joined.
But in eternity: I share too much
Of him that's going thither.

Car. Poor woman, 'twas not thy fault; I grieve to see thee weep for him that hath my pity too.

Win. My fault was lust, my punishment was shame.
Yet I am happy that my soul is free
Both from consent, foreknowledge, and intent
Of any murder but of mine own honour,
Restored again by a fair satisfaction,
And since not to be wounded.

O. Thor. Daughter, grieve not
For what necessity forceth;
Rather resolve to conquer it with patience.—
Alas, she faints!

Win. My griefs are strong upon me;
My weakness scarce can bear them.

[*Within.*] Away with her! hang her, witch!

Enter to execution Mother Sawyer; *Officers with halberds, followed by a crowd of Country-people.*

Car. The witch, that instrument of mischief! Did not she witch the devil into my son-in-law, when he killed my poor daughter? Do you hear, Mother Sawyer?

M. Saw. What would you have?
Cannot a poor old woman have your leave
To die without vexation?

Car. Did not you bewitch Frank to kill his wife? he could never have done't without the devil.

M. Saw. Who doubts it? but is every devil mine?
Would I had one now whom I might command
To tear you all in pieces? Tom would have done't
Before he left me.

Car. Thou didst bewitch Ann Ratcliffe to kill herself.

M. Saw. Churl, thou liest; I never did her hurt:
Would you were all as near your ends as I am,
That gave evidence against me for it!

1st Coun. I'll be sworn, Master Carter, she bewitched Gammer Washbowl's sow to cast her pigs a day before she would have farrowed: yet they were sent up to London and sold for as good Westminster dog-pigs at Bartholomew fair as ever great-bellied ale-wife longed for.

M. Saw. These dogs will mad me: I was well resolved
To die in my repentance. Though 'tis true
I would live longer if I might, yet since
I cannot, pray torment me not; my conscience
Is settled as it shall be: all take heed
How they believe the devil; at last he'll cheat you.

Car. Thou'dst best confess all truly.

M. Saw. Yet again?
Have I scarce breath enough to say my prayers,
And would you force me to spend that in bawling?
Bear witness, I repent all former evil;
There is no damnèd conjuror like the devil.

All. Away with her, away! [*She is led off.*

Enter FRANK *to execution, Officers, &c.*

O. Thor. Here's the sad object which I yet must meet
With hope of comfort, if a repentant end
Make him more happy than misfortune would
Suffer him here to be.

Frank. Good sirs, turn from me:
You will revive affliction almost killed
With my continual sorrow.

O. Thor. O, Frank, Frank!
Would I had sunk in mine own wants, or died
But one bare minute ere thy fault was acted!

Frank. To look upon your sorrows executes me
Before my execution.

Win. Let me pray you, sir—

Frank. Thou much-wronged woman, I must sigh for thee,
As he that's only loth to leave the world
For that he leaves thee in it unprovided,
Unfriended; and for me to beg a pity
From any man to thee when I am gone
Is more than I can hope; nor, to say truth,
Have I deserved it: but there is a payment
Belongs to goodness from the great exchequer
Above; it will not fail thee, Winnifred;
Be that thy comfort.

O. Thor. Let it be thine too,
Untimely-lost young man.

Frank. He is not lost
Who bears his peace within him: had I spun
My web of life out at full length, and dreamed
Away my many years in lusts, in surfeits,
Murders of reputations, gallant sins
Commended or approved; then, though I had
Died easily, as great and rich men do,
Upon my own bed, not compelled by justice,
You might have mourn'd for me indeed; my miseries
Had been as everlasting as remediless:
But now the law hath not arraigned, condemned
With greater rigour my unhappy fact
Than I myself have every little sin
My memory can reckon from my childhood:
A court hath been kept here, where I am found
Guilty; the difference is, my impartial judge
Is much more gracious than my faults

Are monstrous to be named; yet they are monstrous.

O. Thor. Here's comfort in this penitence.

Win. It speaks
How truly you are reconciled, and quickens
My dying comfort, that was near expiring
With my last breath: now this repentance makes thee
As white as innocence; and my first sin with thee,
Since which I knew none like it, by my sorrow
Is clearly cancelled. Might our souls together
Climb to the height of their eternity,
And there enjoy what earth denied us, happiness!
But since I must survive, and be the monument
Of thy loved memory, I will preserve it
With a religious care, and pay thy ashes
A widow's duty, calling that end best
Which, though it stain the name, makes the soul blest.

Frank. Give me thy hand, poor woman; do not weep.
Farewell: thou dost forgive me?

Win. 'Tis my part
To use that language.

Frank. O, that my example
Might teach the world hereafter what a curse
Hangs on their heads who rather choose to marry
A goodly portion than a dower of virtues!—
Are you there, gentlemen? there is not one
Amongst you whom I have not wronged; [*to* CARTER] you most:
I robbed you of a daughter; but she is
In Heaven; and I must suffer for it willingly.

Car. Ay, ay, she's in Heaven, and I am so glad to see thee so well prepared to follow her. I forgive thee with all my heart; if thou hadst not had ill counsel, thou wouldst not have done as thou didst; the more shame for them.

Som. Spare your excuse to me, I do conceive
What you would speak; I would you could as easily
Make satisfaction to the law as to my wrongs.
I am sorry for you.

War. And so am I,

And heartily forgive you.

Kath. I will pray for you
For her sake, who I'm sure did love you dearly.

Sir Arth. Let us part friendly too; I am ashamed
Of my part in thy wrongs.

Frank. You are all merciful,
And send me to my grave in peace. Sir Arthur,
Heaven send you a new heart!—Lastly, to you, sir;
And though I have deserved not to be called
Your son, yet give me leave upon my knees
To beg a blessing. [*Kneels.*

O. Thor. Take it; let me wet
Thy cheeks with the last tears my griefs have left me.
O, Frank, Frank, Frank!

Frank. Let me beseech you, gentlemen,
To comfort my old father, keep him with ye;
Love this distressèd widow; and as often
As you remember what a graceless man
I was, remember likewise that these are
Both free, both worthy of a better fate
Than such a son or husband as I have been.
All help me with your prayers.—On, on; 'tis just
That law should purge the guilt of blood and lust. [*Exit, led off by the Officers.*

Car. Go thy ways; I did not think to have shed one tear for thee, but thou hast made me water my plants spite of my heart.—Master Thorney, cheer up, man; whilst I can stand by you, you shall not want help to keep you from falling: we have lost our children, both on's, the wrong way, but we cannot help it; better or worse, 'tis now as 'tis.

O. Thor. I thank you, sir; you are more kind than I
Have cause to hope or look for.

Car. Master Somerton, is Kate yours or no?

Som. We are agreed.

Kath. And but my faith is passed, I should fear to be married, husbands are so cruelly unkind. Excuse me that I am thus troubled.

Som. Thou shalt have no cause.

Just. Take comfort, Mistress Winnifred: Sir Arthur,
For his abuse to you and to your husband,
Is by the bench enjoined to pay you down
A thousand marks.[52]

Sir Arth. Which I will soon discharge.

Win. Sir, 'tis too great a sum to be employed
Upon my funeral.

Car. Come, come; if luck had served, Sir Arthur, and every man had his due, somebody might have tottered ere this, without paying fines, like it as you list.—Come to me, Winnifred; shalt be welcome.—Make much of her, Kate, I charge you: I do not think but she's a good wench, and hath had wrong as well as we. So let's every man home to Edmonton with heavy hearts, yet as merry as we can, though not as we would.

Just. Join, friends, in sorrow; make of all the best:
Harms past may be lamented, not redrest. [*Exeunt.*

[52]The mark was worth 13*s.* 4*d.*

EPILOGUE

Spoken by WINNIFRED.

I am a widow still, and must not sort
A second choice without a good report;
Which though some widows find, and few deserve,
Yet I dare not presume, but will not swerve
From modest hopes. All noble tongues are free;
The gentle may speak one kind word for me.

Phen.

FINIS

Made in the USA
Middletown, DE
12 August 2024